TELEVISION, THE BOOK, AND THE CLASSROOM

A Seminar Cosponsored by the
Center for the Book in the Library of Congress
and the U.S. Office of Education
and Held at the Library of Congress on
April 26-27, 1978

Edited by
John Y. Cole

The Center for the Book

Library of Congress   Washington 1978

Library of Congress Cataloging in Publication Data

Main entry under title:

Television, the book, and the classroom.

1. Television in education—United States—Congresses.
2. Books and reading—United States—Congresses.
3. Educational technology—United States—Congresses.
I. Cole, John Young, 1940-   II. Center for the Book.
III. United States. Office of Education.

LB1044.7.T36   371.3'078   78-23543
ISBN 0-8444-0303-2

For sale by the Information Office,
Library of Congress
Washington, D.C. 20540

CONTENTS

INTRODUCTION

On April 26 and 27, 1978, the Library of Congress and the U.S. Office of Education cosponsored a national seminar on television, the book, and the classroom. This collaborative effort between two government agencies had a purpose that runs counter to much of contemporary public comment about television. Books such as *The Plug-In Drug* by Marie Winn, *Remote Control: Television and the Manipulation of American Life* by Frank Mankiewicz and Joel Swerdlow, *Four Arguments for the Elimination of Television* by Jerry Mander, and *The Sponsor: Notes on a Modern Potentate* by Erik Barnouw have contributed to a general unhappiness about television and its effect on American society and culture.

The organizers of the seminar took a more positive view and assumed that television could, should, and eventually would be used effectively in the educational process. Seminar participants were asked to address these questions:

> How can television be used imaginatively and effectively in the learning process?
>
> What practical steps can be taken at the national level to integrate television, the book, and the printed word within the educational process?

The stated purpose of the seminar was "to stimulate fresh thinking and perhaps new partnerships" among the participants, with a special emphasis on the potential role of commercial television. Both public television and the commercial networks were represented. Other

1

participants included educators, publishers, government officials, scholars, librarians, and parent groups.

Two pioneers in their respective fields, Mortimer J. Adler and Frank Stanton, were asked to deliver brief keynote addresses on April 26. Their effectiveness can be gauged by the many references to their talks during the meetings on April 27. On that day seminar participants also heard the views of six individuals who represented different segments of American society. These speakers were asked to look ahead and describe what needed to be done rather than to criticize what had or had not been done. They were asked to look beyond the contemporary criticism of television and toward the day when the special qualities of television and of the written word would be combined—especially for the benefit of young people.

Of course it is far too early to judge whether a seminar based on such sanguine hopes has achieved any lasting results. The Office of Education and the Library of Congress are continuing their catalytic roles. The Office of Education's request for proposals to integrate television and books more effectively into the educational process, announced during the seminar (see pages 90–91), has produced many interesting and original plans. The Center for the Book in the Library of Congress, which cosponsored the seminar as part of its concern about the future of the printed word in relation to new technologies and other media, is cosponsoring two other conferences during the coming year that will explore different aspects of television's impact on books and reading. In October 1978 it will join with the Book Industry Study Group, Inc. for a seminar on American reading and book-buying habits, and in May 1979 it will cosponsor, with the National Institute of Education, a conference on "The Textbook in American Education."

The new partnership reflected here grew out of a mutual concern of two thoughtful, articulate, and, in civil service terms, relatively inexperienced government

2

officials: Ernest L. Boyer, who became U.S. Commissioner of Education on April 1, 1977, and Daniel J. Boorstin, who has been Librarian of Congress since November 12, 1975. The editor of this volume gratefully acknowledges their support, along with the help provided by Peggy Rhoades, Assistant Commissioner for Public Affairs, Office of Education, and Martin Kaplan, Executive Assistant to the Commissioner of Education. In addition, special thanks go to John Platt, Lecturer in the Departments of Anthropology and Environmental Studies at the University of California at Santa Barbara, and Jean Johnson, Resource Director for Action for Children's Television, whose contributions appear as Appendixes 2 and 3, respectively.

John Y. Cole
Executive Director
The Center for the Book
August 1978

APRIL 26

OPENING REMARKS

DANIEL J. BOORSTIN,
THE LIBRARIAN OF CONGRESS

Welcome, ladies and gentlemen, to the first national conference sponsored by the Center for the Book in the Library of Congress. You have all been invited here tonight because of your special interest in this question, and I will speak for only a moment or two about the focus of our interest this evening.

We are here to help us discover or rediscover America, which we can do only by understanding the place of technology in our lives. One of the most interesting and most important questions concerning the place of technology in our civilization is the effect of one technology on another.

The relationship among innovations and inventions is one of the least understood and one of the most momentous questions in the history of humankind. It is also an area for the greatest flights of fancy, the greatest alarmists and Armaggedon-mongers and the most extravagant utopians and optimists.

Nowhere is this more evident than in the relationship between television and the book. We have here, in this question of the relationship between the technology of television and the book, a melodramatic example of what I would call the displacive fallacy, the fallacy that an invention is a conqueror and makes the predecessor surrender. This is not so. As we discover in our own experience, each technology transforms the earlier one. For example, the telephone transformed the role of the telegraph, and radio and the telephone transformed the roles of all earlier technologies.

There were some prophets who said that the radio

7

would obsolete the telephone because no one would want to communicate with a wire if he could avoid it and that the phonograph would obsolete orchestras and all forms of handmade music. But we know that the automobile has not obsoleted the bicycle. Television and the radio have not obsoleted the press. The automobile, despite some of the fears expressed, has not obsoleted the human body, although it has been observed that, if God had intended man to walk, he would have given him wheels.

This is one of the questions that we are concerned with here tonight and tomorrow. We are here to explode and to explore the displacive fallacy, to explore the complementarity of technologies. We are inclined to forget that there are many historical features which television and the book have in common.

We forget that the book was a triumph of technology and that the book was considered to be a mechanical manuscript just as television is sometimes considered to be an audiovisual book. We forget also that both these new technologies were and are highly suspect by academics and by the aristocracy of learning. There were many people who did not want to have a machine-made book and preferred the manuscript, just as there are some people today who will not have a television set in their homes "until it is perfected."

Both these technologies, the book and television, have gargantuanly multiplied our experience. Tonight and tomorrow we will see their community. We will explore their complementarity with the aid of the people who have been concerned with both of them.

I have mentioned that this is the first national seminar sponsored by the Library's new Center for the Book. We are especially pleased that it is being co-sponsored with the Office of Education and that it concerns such a vital topic as that which we will be focusing on this evening.

The Center for the Book was established by act of Congress last year. Its general purpose is to enhance the appreciation of the book and its fundamental relationship to development of our civilization. It will, we hope, serve as a catalyst in the book world and the educational world and the world of television.

We will work with and through organizations. We will reach out to encourage the use of books, the study of books, the reading of books, to examine the question of what we mean by reading, to explore the cultural and technological issues related to the future of books and of reading.

It is the question of the future of books and of reading in the age of television and the future of television in the age of the book that brings us here tonight. The purpose of our seminar is to bring together several segments of our society—those who are interested in commercial and in public television, educators, the communications industry, publishers, book people, and just citizens—to explore new opportunities and to help create new opportunities. Before we are finished with our session tomorrow, I hope we will have begun to do something more to integrate television and the printed word within the educational process.

It gives me pleasure now, a special pleasure, to introduce to you a cosponsor of our sessions this evening and tomorrow, United States Commissioner of Education Ernest Boyer, who will share with me the duties of moderator of our sessions tomorrow and who will help me chair the sessions this evening.

OPENING REMARKS

ERNEST L. BOYER,
U.S. COMMISSIONER OF EDUCATION

In the summer of 1937, the great essayist and novelist E. B. White sat transfixed in a darkened room and watched a big electronic box that began projecting eerie, shimmering images into the world. It was his first introduction to something called TV. E. B. White —who not only wrote *Charlotte's Web* but also co-authored that great manual of clear communication *The Elements of Style*—said in 1938:

"I believe television is going to be the test of the modern world, and that in this new opportunity to see beyond the range of our vision we shall discover either a new and unbearable disturbance of the general peace, or a saving radiance in the sky. We shall stand or fall by television—of that I am quite sure."

Forty years have passed and television has to a remarkable degree fulfilled both of E. B. White's predictions. It has—at once—become both "an unbearable disturbance" *and* "a soaring radiance in the sky." Once we had a print-dominated culture. Ideas were built and assimilated slowly, and often with great effort. Now we inhabit a culture of images. Messages are sent and received instantaneously, and a premium is placed on the accessible. And what are we to make of all of this? How do we come to terms—educationally—with a world where messages have become more persistent and more varied?

When I was young, less than fifty years ago, there was no television in our home. I was twelve years old before we purchased our first radio. We did receive a

11

daily newspaper and the *National Geographic*, which I eagerly devoured as soon as it arrived. Our Model A took us on short excursions from our Ohio home, rarely more than one hundred miles or so. As I look back on those early years, school was the central learning place. The teacher—for better or for worse—was the key source of knowledge, and the classroom was the intellectual window to the world. (It was only later that I learned just how clouded that window could sometimes be.)

For students coming to our schools today, that world I knew is ancient history. Today the first thing to captivate the infant in the cradle is probably that iridescent, inexhaustible screen. At least one study has shown that, by the age of three, children are purposeful viewers who can name their favorite programs. Young children—two to five years old—now watch television over four hours every day, nearly thirty hours a week. That's more than fifteen hundred hours every year. And by the time a youngster enters first grade he or she has had six thousand hours of television viewing. This same TV saturation continues after school begins. By the time of high school graduation, the average child will have spent *thirty per cent more time watching television than in school.* Today, the traditional teacher is not the only source of knowledge. The school has become almost incidental to some students. The classroom has less impact and receives less respect. To put it bluntly, a new electronic "classroom" has emerged.

Several years ago, our young son, who had just entered kindergarten, said the alphabet one night when he went to bed—rather than his prayers. At the end, I complimented him for having recited the alphabet without a hitch—even though he had been in kindergarten just one week. He replied by saying: Actually, I learned the alphabet on *Sesame Street*—but my kindergarten teacher thinks she taught it to me. I was delighted. My son had not only learned the alphabet;

12

he had learned the system, too!

My *National Geographic*—which gave me glimpses of the outside world—has today been smothered by an avalanche of publications—some good, some bad—which open up new worlds to students. Today, paperbacks, magazines, television, and travel compete on equal footing with the classroom and the book. Today—for better or for worse—Archie Bunker is better known than Silas Marner, Fellini is more influential than Faulkner, and the six o'clock news is more compelling than the history text.

It seems quite clear to me that the separate sources of information which educate our children must somehow be brought together. Surely this so-called standoff between the classroom and TV reflects our narrowness rather than our vision. Surely, the various sources of information need not be in competition with each other. Surely, our job as communicators as well as educators is to recognize the world has changed, to rejoice in the marvel of expanding knowledge, and to find ways to relate the classroom more closely to the networks of information beyond the classroom.

BOOKS, TELEVISION, AND LEARNING

MORTIMER J. ADLER

The letter I received from Mr. Boyer describing this occasion posed three questions to which he hoped I would address myself. From the way in which the questions were worded, slanted in the direction of the bookish member of this evening's little duet, I suspect that the questions put to Mr. Stanton were somewhat different. In any case, I liked the questions put to me and I would like to try to answer them. The three questions were:

First, what is the place of the book in a television society?

Second, what special qualities of the book ensure its central role in the learning process?

Third, how has television—the hours we spend with it and its content—affected our relations with books, with schooling, and with learning?

The second of these three questions seems to me to be the pivotal question and, therefore, I will deal with it first and with the remaining two questions later. The second question, as worded, appears to assume the superiority of the book in the learning process—whether in school or after all schooling is completed. Please note, Mr. Stanton, that the question does not ask *whether* the book occupies a central role in the learning process. It asks *why* the book occupies that role. If the assumption here being made—that the book is indispensable to the learning process, as television is not—is doubted or challenged by anyone, then my

15

first task is certainly to show why that assumption is thoroughly justified.

To do so with fairness to television, we are obligated to deal with all three elements under consideration at their very best. Not all books are good books; in fact most are not, as most television is not very good. In addition, schooling in this country at present is probably at its lowest ebb, and the state of adult learning is equally deplorable. It would be unfair to proceed as if the schools are doing the job they should be doing, and as if books are serving the purpose they should be serving, and then to consider television against the background of suppositions so contrary to fact. No, we must compare books at their very best with television at its very best in relation to schooling and the learning process as they should be, not as they are.

To make the comparison in that way, which seems to me the only fair way to make it, I think it is necessary, first, to summarize briefly the educational ideal appropriate to our kind of society—a technologically advanced industrial democracy (in order to be quite explicit about what schooling and learning should be like in our society); and then to state the three functions that books perform (in order to indicate the three respects in which television and books should be compared). I will proceed at once to these two preliminary matters, after which I will make the threefold comparison that will explain the superiority of books in relation to the learning process, in school or out of it, then deal with the two remaining questions that Mr. Boyer's letter posed, and finally state a few conclusions.

What should schooling and the learning process be like in our kind of society (an ideal that is far from being realized at present)? Elitism in any shape or form must be rejected, not only for the educational process itself but also for the use of books and of television. A society dedicated to universal suffrage and one in which technologically advanced industrialization provides every citizen with ample free time for the pur-

16

suits of leisure (preeminent among which is learning) is a society that should be dedicated to the principle of equal educational opportunity for all—all without exception. This calls not only for the same amount of basic schooling for all but also for the same quality of basic schooling for all—completely liberal schooling for all, without any trace of vocational training in it.

Such basic schooling should begin at age four and terminate at age sixteen with the B.A. degree. It should not aim to turn out educated or learned men and women, for that is an impossible task for the school to perform. Children cannot be made learned, any more than they can be made wise; for immaturity is an insuperable obstacle to both. But children can be made competent as learners, and they can be introduced to the world of learning and given the motivation to continue learning after they have left school. If our schools and colleges—up to the B.A. degree—did nothing else, they would be doing the very best that can be expected of them.

Schooling at its very best is only the beginning of the educational process. At its best, it is only a preparation for a lifetime of continued learning, which may ultimately produce an educated man or woman. It provides such preparation to the extent that it inculcates the liberal arts, which are the arts of learning—the skills of reading, writing, speaking, listening, observing, measuring, and calculating. These are the arts of thinking as well, for there is no genuine learning (learning that is better than rote memory) which does not involve thinking. Learning does not consist in the passive reception of content that is committed to memory and regurgitated at some later time. It is not the activity of the teacher that is essential to learning, but the activity of the learner—intellectual activity that involves acts of understanding that involve the consideration of ideas. That is why Socrates always represents the ideal teacher, one who teaches by asking, not by telling, one who demands intellectual activity on the

17

part of the learner, not passive reception.

So much for what schooling and learning should be, ideally. Now let me turn to the other of my two preliminary considerations—the three functions that books perform, with respect to which a comparison with television can be made. In *How To Read A Book*, first published almost forty years ago, I distinguished three different aims that we may have when we resort to books.

Our aim may be simply entertainment—at the lowest level, merely to pass away the time, for recreation or relaxation, for getting drowsy enough to go to sleep—and at higher levels, entertainment to engage our minds a little more than that, but nevertheless falling short of instructing us or elevating our minds. A second aim may be the acquirement of information or, beyond that, instruction in some field of organized knowledge.

The third purpose that books may serve is to improve our minds, not merely with respect to knowledge, but beyond that with respect to insight and understanding. Let me describe this third use of books as the process whereby the reading of books that are over our head enables us to lift our minds up from the state of understanding less to the state of understanding more. This third use of books need not exclude the first or second. Reading books for the sake of enlightenment may be pleasurable and entertaining; it may also be informative or instructive; but it is never merely that.

The rules set forth in *How To Read A Book*—and the liberal arts that will be acquired by following these rules—apply only to reading books for the third of these three purposes. They are not necessary for books read merely for entertainment, nor even for books read merely for information or factual instruction. Furthermore, there are only a few books worth reading for the sake of genuinely improving the mind, only a few that deserve the care and effort required by the rules set forth in *How To Read A Book*. Of the thirty-five or

18

forty thousand books published in the United States each year, how many would you say deserve such careful and effortful reading? My estimate is less than a thousand. And of that thousand, how many deserve a second equally careful reading? Probably less than a hundred. And more than two careful readings—merely a handful at most. The last thing in the world that I am saying is that most books are good and most television is bad. On the contrary, I am saying very few books are good for the learning process as it should be carried on.

Let us begin the comparison of books and television by considering them with respect to a purpose both obviously serve—the purpose of providing entertainment. Here it seems to me we are all compelled to admit that TV at its best is about as good as books at their very best. It may be argued that the great novels and the great plays that have been produced on television are necessarily somewhat diminished in scope and substance by the exigencies of that medium. To this extent there may be more entertainment provided by books than by television. On the other hand, it can be said that the vividness of television—the power of verbal and pictorial narration combined as compared with the power of merely verbal narration—gives the superiority to television. However, for our present purpose, since we are concerned with the learning process, not with entertainment, we need not decide whether reading a play by Shakespeare or a novel by Dostoievski is superior to seeing it on the stage or on the TV screen.

Next, let us consider books and television as conveyors of information and as instruments of factual instruction. Here, again, books and television come out about equal. Here, again, each may have superiority in one respect but not in another. It is, further, appropriate to consider here the role that educational films and educational television can play in the classroom. Considering them, as they are usually considered, as audiovisual aids, they are just that and no more. To say that they are just audiovisual aids is to say that, in the learning process, properly carried on, they must be supplemented by other materials or means of learning: by the effort of the teacher, which at its best should consist in asking questions and conducting discussion, and by books that, at their very best—filled with illustrations, diagrams, maps, and so forth—can do the whole job almost as well as it can be done without resort to audiovisual aids. But it may be said that teaching films and teaching television may go beyond being audiovisual aids. They may be primary and independent sources of instruction and information about matters of fact. But even when they are so considered and, in addition, are as good as they can possibly be, they are no better than lectures delivered by a first-rate lecturer, accompanied in some instances by laboratory demonstrations, by slides, by charts, maps, and diagrams. To which I must add one further point; namely, that the best lecture is only second-best as a means of instruction, inferior to the Socratic procedure of asking questions and conducting discussion.

Finally, we come to the third purpose that books—the best books, I should say—can serve: the reading of books for the purpose of improving the mind by enlightening it, by activating the thinking process, by awakening ideas in it, by elevating it from understanding less to understanding more. Here television and books are incomparable, for books, or at least some books, the best books, can perform this function for those who have learned how to read, and television cannot perform this function at all. Precisely because only books can perform this function, books and books alone require the learner to become disciplined in the liberal arts, the arts of reading and discussion, of asking questions and pursuing the answers to them. If there were no books—a contrafactual supposition that I hope our television society never turns into a statement of fact, if television were in fact the only medium of communication, there would be no occasion in the learning process, in school or out of it, for the acquirements of the liberal arts. Television may, in some rare instances, stimulate thinking, but it does not demand much skill in thinking, nor does it cultivate such skill. If books were not used in the learning process, and if our teachers fell far short of the power of Socrates (who cultivated the liberal arts without resort to books), I cannot imagine how or where in the learning process the liberal arts would be acquired, or how and where the mind would be enlightened by abstract ideas or disciplined in the skill of dealing with them. This, and this alone, is my basic challenge to Mr. Stanton as the exponent of television in this discussion. If he cannot meet it, then I rest my case. If he tries to, then I will resume my effort to show that he is wrong.

What is the place of the book in a television society? That is a factual, not a theoretical, question. The answer to it is that, in our television society, television has more and more resulted in the displacement of books in the learning process, not only for the young in school but for their elders in adult life. Why is this so? Why is it likely to be increasingly true? First, because there is a limited amount of free time at our disposal to use well or poorly. There is only so much of it; and if television preempts more and more of it, less and less of it will remain for the reading of books. Second, because of the weakness of the flesh, which naturally tends to take the easier path, the less effortful, the less strenuous. The more pleasurable and painless, the less active and effortful, will always tend to displace that which involves the painful effort required to learn by thinking.

I will have more to say on this point, presently, when, in my concluding remarks, I will comment on the pain of learning, a pain that all of us must have the courage to suffer in order to do what we should do for our minds. For the moment, I want to qualify what I have just said about the unfortunate effects that television has had in the displacement of books. The fault does not lie primarily with television. If the schools were doing the job they should be doing, if they were giving the young the liberal training they should provide, they would themselves act as the needed countervailing force to counteract the enticements of television. The failure of the schools is the primary cause of the displacement of books by television. If the schools did their job properly, books would still reign supreme even in a television society.

The one remaining question is: how has television —the hours we spend with it and its content—affected our relations with books, with schooling, and with learning? The basic point I want to make here concerns the habit of mind that watching television cultivates. It is a habit of passive reception, sitting back and letting the bewitching images on the screen wash over one. This passive habit of mind is then transferred to the reading of books, which results in the kind of reading that does not deserve the name; for passive reading is not reading at all in any sense that is appropriate to the use of the best books for the enlightenment, elevation, and improvement of the mind.

This happens not only to children in school, who read passively, not actively, even the relatively poor books that they are assigned to read in the degraded curriculums that now prevail everywhere, not only in our high schools but also in our colleges. Little profit results from sitting down with a book, turning the pages, and letting its contents wash over the mind in the same way that one sits back and succumbs passively to television. When books are read in this way, they might just as well not be read at all, except to memorize for the sake of regurgitating the memorized content on examinations and then forgetting it. Certainly new ideas, new insights, better understanding cannot be acquired in this way. No thinking is involved and, therefore, little if any genuine learning.

Let me repeat what I have already said. Television

22

cannot be blamed for the failure of the schools to do what they should do, even if it can be said that the amount of time consumed in watching television and the bad habit of mind that watching television forms make it more difficult for schools and teachers to do what they should be doing. Nor can television be blamed for the most widespread of all American misconceptions about learning—that it should all be fun, that if it cannot be made effortlessly pleasant, it should be avoided or only minimally endured.

To amplify this last point, I would like to conclude this address by quoting from an essay that I wrote in 1941. At that time, I had in mind the two very best educational programs on radio. One was the University of Chicago's Round Table; the other was a radio program—on CBS, I believe—called "Invitation to Learning," conducted by two friends of mine, Mark Van Doren and Lyman Bryson. Both of these programs involved the discussion of important ideas and issues and, in the case of "Invitation to Learning," the discussion of good books. Both resulted in the distribution on request to listeners of transcripts of the program. These transcripts always included bibliographies of recommended books to be read. Both programs regarded themselves as occasions for further learning by the reading of books.

The title of the essay I wrote in 1941 was "Invitation to the Pain of Learning." The brunt of its criticism was directed at the schools, at the educators, and at the American public in general. The fundamental mistake being made by all of them, I tried to say, was their fallacious supposition that all learning should be fun, should be effortless and easy, not only in the classroom but throughout the whole of life. I have brought along with me copies of this paper that I will distribute to the conferees tomorrow morning. Now I will confine myself to quoting its concluding paragraphs:

"I do not know whether radio or television will ever be able to do anything genuinely educative. I am sure it serves the public in two ways: by giving them amusement and by giving them information. It may even, as in the case of its very best "educational" programs, stimulate some persons to do something about their minds by pursuing knowledge and wisdom in the only way possible—the hard way. But what I do not know is whether it can ever do what the best teachers have always done and must now be doing; namely, to present programs which are genuinely educative, as opposed to merely stimulating, in the sense that following them requires the listener to be active not passive, to think rather than remember, and to suffer all the pains of lifting himself up by his own bootstraps.

"Certainly so long as the so-called educational directors of our leading networks continue to operate on their present false principles, we can expect nothing. So long as they confuse education and entertainment, so long as they suppose that learning can be accomplished without pain, so long as they persist in bringing everything and everybody down to the lowest level on which the largest audience can be reached, the educational programs offered on the air will remain what they are today—shams and delusions.

"It may be, of course, that the radio and television, for economic reasons must, like the motion picture, reach with certainty so large an audience that the networks cannot afford even to experiment with programs which make no pretense to be more palatable and pleasurable than real education can be. It may be that the radio and television cannot be expected to take a sounder view of education and to undertake more substantial programs than now prevail among the country's official leaders in education—the heads of our school system, of our colleges, of our adult education associations. But, in either case, let us not fool ourselves about what we are doing.

" 'Education' all wrapped up in attractive tissue is the gold brick that is being sold in America today on every street corner. Every one is selling it, every one is buying it, but no one is giving or getting the real thing because the real thing is always hard to give or get. Yet the real thing can be made generally available if the obstacles to its distribution are honestly recognized. Unless we acknowledge that every invitation to learning can promise pleasure only as the result of pain, can offer achievement only at the expense of work, all of our invitations to learning, in school and out, whether by books, lectures, or radio and television programs will be as much buncombe as the worst patent medicine advertising, or the campaign pledge to put two chickens in every pot."

TELEVISION AND THE BOOK

FRANK STANTON

Our presence here tonight is testimony to a significant truth, one we all applaud. It clearly demonstrates once again that this illustrious institution is not a mere book collector, a storehouse of what has been done, but that it is an activist in the promotion of things yet to come. In establishing the Center for the Book six months ago, Congress created a fresh advocate of the printed word as a vital element of American culture. This first public seminar, conducted with the U. S. Office of Education, sets the Center on a course which should greatly enhance our national life.

It is reassuring to me that this seminar pairs the first instrument of mass communication growing out of technological progress with the most recent. The book, made generally available by Gutenberg's ingenuity, has been an important instrument of education over the past five centuries. I believe television now has an equally important educational role, and I am persuaded that a partnership of the two will enrich all levels of American culture in future centuries.

That phrase, "all levels of American culture," is a crucial one in this discussion, for books and television both are ubiquitous. Television is a nearly universal medium of communication, and books also penetrate a wide span of national life. Both are involved in informing, entertaining and educating people at all social and economic levels. They must meet the demands of diversity as well as mass appeal.

Television is a newcomer to our mass communications mix. Although the technology was developed a half century ago, it did not come into wide public use until after World War II. At the beginning of 1948, there were 15 television stations on the air and they could be received in 200,000 homes. Ten years later, we had 520 stations reaching 42 million homes. That was the decade of explosive growth; the trend has been somewhat more sedate in the subsequent decades.

Today, there are television sets in 73 million households, and those homes account for 204 million Americans. That is about 97 percent of the total population and probably is as close as you can come to a universal system of public communication. The time spent viewing television also has been increasing. It rose a half hour between the 1970-71 season and the 1976-77 season, when people were averaging three hours and forty-eight minutes per day.

Consider what is involved in attracting our fellow citizens to their sets for that much viewing. The networks and the individual stations together present material to fill eighteen to twenty-four hours of broadcasting, 365 days of the year. They report the news and, through documentaries, analyze the major issues of the day. They present thoughtful dramatic productions and exciting sports events. And they must come up with a schedule of the comedy and action adventure which permits people to relax from the tensions of life. All of this, of course, must have sufficient range and variety to appeal to all of the highly diverse segments of contemporary society.

Eric Sevareid tells an illuminating story about an hour of talk with Hugo Black, who was the first sitting Supreme Court justice to agree to a lengthy interview on television. Eric calls it a fascinating hour with a beautiful mind. Yet when it was broadcast, another network featured an hour with Brigitte Bardot. Most of the audience preferred another kind of beauty that day, for Mlle Bardot won the ratings contest hands down. The point is that we must continue to have the Justice Blacks as well as the Mlles Bardots on the air

28

because television must serve the audiences that will find each of them appealing.

In the course of pursuing the goal of universal appeal through diversity, television naturally will be producing material somebody doesn't like. And in the course of constantly creating new material to fill those twenty-four hours each day of the year, there will be some mistakes, some lapses of taste, some banality. It is inevitable and it gives rise to considerable criticism. I would not defend everything that appears on television, but I do believe that the medium by and large does a good job of meeting the varied responsibilities of mass public communications.

I also hear some echoes from the world of books during an analogous stage of development. When the United States was little more than a half century old, Alexis de Tocqueville said of our democratic populace that "they prefer books which may be easily procured, quickly read and which require no learned researches to be understood. The ever increasing crowd of readers, and their continual craving for something new, ensure the sale of books that nobody much esteems." Viewpoints on communications don't seem to change much from century to century.

I imagine that when Gutenberg introduced his machine, the new technology sent a shudder through the intellectual world of the time. What would it do to the established tradition of creating and transmitting wisdom? What of the sages and teachers, the oracles and preachers who had carried civilization that far? Their works had been stored away on stone, papyrus, and parchment where they were accessible to priests and scholars. But what would happen when knowledge was accessible to the masses? We are here tonight to celebrate the fact that printing has worked out quite well for mankind, so well we are convinced that books should be promoted for an even stronger role in the future.

What are the prospects for books now that a new

communications technology has captured the public fancy? If the record is any indication, the prospects are excellent. Let's take a quick look at the quarter century between 1950 and 1975, the time when television developed into a major force in this society. During that period, the population grew 43 percent, but the number of book titles published in this country more than tripled. They rose from eighty-six hundred in 1950 to thirty thousand in 1975, and by now the total is fast approaching forty thousand. Sales of the ubiquitous paperback book increased ten times, going from $44 million to $450 million.

There were gains in periodical publishing, too. The number of daily newspapers stayed at about seventeen hundred, but circulation rose from 54 million to 61 million. In addition to newspapers, there were sixty-nine hundred periodicals of all types published in 1950, while by 1975 there were ninety-six hundred and they ranged from broad national publications to the narrowest of special interests.

All of this tells us we should resist the temptation to label our times the Age of Television. It really is an era of mass communication. Ours is not a television society but one in which attitudes and ambitions are shaped by information and impressions from all kinds of sources. People might spend three or four hours watching television, but they spend another twelve waking hours working, talking, reading, traveling. It is this total experience that creates the sense of reality, and I am rather impatient with the notion occasionally expressed that the ordinary citizen is weakminded to the point that a few hours of television each day can turn him into a video-guided vegetable.

Books have a very strong role in the process of mass communication. Anybody who strolls through a drug store, airport, or supermarket knows that the day of the book as an erudite object between hard covers has long since gone. The image of books as the talisman of a privileged minority or an intellectual elite is

30

a thing of the fading past, and that is a very healthy development in a democratic society. Books of all sizes, shapes, and content are found everywhere, thanks in good part to the advent of the paperback. They are a source of ideas and enjoyment for scores of millions of our citizens. These volumes do not all have serious content or lofty themes, since they must appeal to a wide range of interests, tastes, moods, and levels of comprehension. But the important fact is that people are reading.

That there is a positive correlation between increased television viewing and the increased use of books surprises some people. Perhaps they remember the days twenty-five years ago when the advent of television did put a dent in the public's reading habits. During the early fifties, library circulation turned downward, and so did book sales. But the trend was soon reversed, and both indicators have risen to new highs in the past two decades. Public library circulation rose from 543 million in 1950 to 927 million twenty-five years later.

The same sort of thing happened in the music world when radio came on the scene. It was feared that the new broadcast medium would destroy the recorded music business, but we now know that the two of them have prospered mightily together.

What happened with television was that it became a part of and contributed to a general explosion in cultural interests. Instead of absorbing the exclusive attention of the public, television stimulated people's interests in all kinds of subjects. Quincy Mumford, who was Librarian of Congress during much of that period, queried his fellow librarians about the impact of television and found a consensus that it stimulated calls for books which were related to programs people had seen. Publishers discovered the same phenomenon.

We discovered the correlation twenty years ago when Channel 2 in New York City broadcast an early morning program called "Sunrise Semester." There

31

was a lecture on Stendhal's *The Red and the Black*, a book which had sold a total of three thousand copies over a seven-year period. Suddenly there was a run on the book stores, and five thousand copies were sold during the three days following the lecture, just in the New York City area.

Much the same thing has happened many times in the intervening years. We received dramatic confirmation of the phenomenon last fall when John Ehrlichman's novel *The Company* was broadcast in the form of a miniseries called "Washington: Behind Closed Doors." Pocket Books printed a special edition of the novel with the television series title prominently displayed on the cover. It is reported that 80 million people watched part or all of the series, and the publisher sold 1.5 million copies of his book.

A strong linkage has developed between books and television during the years between those two events. I think the relationship is worth examining. It involves programs which have come from books and books which have come from programs. It involves the encouragement of writers. And finally it involves the promotion of books simply as a matter of stimulating sales.

I would like to examine the latter point first, not because we are concerned here with the financial fate of publishers but because increased book sales mean increased use of books. It means more people are reading and learning, a matter that certainly does warrant our interest.

Interviewing an author on the air has long been regarded as a technique that benefits viewers, authors, and publishers. Writers are interesting people, and they often bring a lively wit and fresh ideas to the broadcasts which feature them. In turn, television exposure has become a reliable spur to book sales. The "Today" show is generally regarded as the most effective platform, but there are other national and local shows which regularly feature authors discussing their works.

In more recent years, the value of advertising books on television has become apparent. This interest has coincided with the creation of mass distribution systems which broaden public access to books far beyond the traditional system of about five thousand book stores which once prevailed. Supermarkets alone offer nearly fifteen thousand sales outlets, and they are joined by drug stores, convenience food chains, and a great variety of other retail places. Publishers are beginning to commit advertising budgets of as much as $300,000 to move a single title through this system, and the broadly based selling power of television is seen as an effective tool for attracting large audiences for new books.

On the creative side, there is a flow in both directions between the television and publishing worlds. Books have long been a source of material for television, but the pace of adaptations has stepped up in recent years. The development of the miniseries, in which a book is serialized over several successive days, has brought us books like Leon Uris's *QBVII* and Irwin Shaw's *Rich Man, Poor Man.* And, of course, it brought us the phenomenal *Roots.*

We also have seen more traditional shows and series made from Graves's *I, Claudius,* O'Connor's *The Last Hurrah,* Tolkien's *The Hobbit,* and Tolstoy's *Anna Karenina.* The networks currently have more than thirty projects under way to adapt books into television programs over the next two years. And the evidence indicates that those programs not only will entertain their viewers but will stimulate an interest in the books involved. Sales of *I, Claudius* and *Anna Karenina* boomed when they were linked with the television programs.

The story of "Roots" was even more impressive. An audience of 109 million saw at least part of the series, which was broadcast at a time when the book was available in a hardcover edition with a cover price of $12.50. The public response was phenomenal, and

Doubleday has printed 1,575,000 copies of that edition. When Dell Publishing brought the paperback version out later in the year, 2.4 million were printed initially and the advance orders exceeded the press run by 50 percent before delivery.

Books flow in the other direction, too. When a television program is successful, we find the story can be converted into a book which will make its message available to an additional audience over an extended period of time. "Holocaust," seen by an estimated cumulative audience of 109 million, is a prime example. The original television story was written by Gerald Green, a distiguished author with eighteen books to his credit. Then he was commissioned to write a companion book, and Bantam Books had 1,150,000 copies of the paperback edition in print before the program was broadcast. "Holocaust" told a story that is crucial for society to remember, and the companion book will expand greatly the impact of the television program.

The experience with "Holocaust" follows a pattern established by earlier television series of evident cultural value. Public television alone has spawned series which have included "Alistair Cooke's America," "Civilisation" by Kenneth Clark, and "The Ascent of Man" by Jacob Bronowski. They all became bestsellers, as did the book based on "The Adams Chronicles." I think we will see more of this in both public and commercial television. It is an effective joining of the distinctive mass communications capabilities of broadcasting and publishing.

While serving the interest of the public, the increased activity also benefits writers. Television has long offered an additional market for the work of writers formerly limited to the printed word. The flowering synergy between television and publishing should further expand the market for their work. Television has also been the source of substantial sums which encourage the development of writing talent.

In reviewing some of the material sent out by the

Center for the Book, I was particularly interested in a special television issue of the magazine *The National Elementary Principal*. It contains a series of thoughtful articles on the relationship between education and television which reflect many viewpoints found in society. Some fear television, while others despise it. Some are resigned to working with television, and a few are even enthusiastic about the potential contribution to learning. A paper by John Platt of the University of California at Santa Barbara, which accompanied the magazine, even advocates a complete overhaul of the educational system to take full recognition of the revolution electronic technology has wrought in the ways we live and learn. It is clear that there is little consensus about television and that relatively little is being done to take advantage of it.

Perhaps the magazine's editorial expresses it best. It says: "If we consider television viewing as another social problem to be taken on by the schools, we will fail to accomplish much of anything. A better approach . . . would be to regard television as an important, creative, even indispensable instructional tool." The editor, Paul L. Houts, went on to say that there should be a bigger effort to "prepare principals and teachers not only to use instructional television wisely, but to tap the educational opportunities that commercial television offers . . . in the classroom, in the school, we ought to be moving toward making television an integral part of the instructional program." In this connection, it is worth recalling that schools generally failed to make effective use of eight and sixteen millimeter film technology. Let's hope they will take full advantage of the potential of television.

There are two aspects to the role of television in our system of education. One involves the use of television in the classroom. The other is the broader process, which I will discuss later, by which our citizens use television to gain the information and perspective that are vital to a functioning democracy.

Let me first review the ways in which television can serve as an instructional tool in the classroom. One is the use of closed circuit systems to instruct students through a medium they have become comfortable with in their homes. It can be used live, but more often it makes use of prerecorded programs on videotape. The programs can be prepared by specialists and used in conjunction with lesson plans tailored to the needs of students at all levels. The key element, of course, is programming. The technology accomplishes nothing if it is not matched by an intelligent and constructive effort to prepare effective lectures and demonstrations.

A second tool, which supplements the first, is the broadcasting of educational programs to the schools. Many public television stations across the country, as well as a few other noncommercial outlets, schedule a full complement of educational programs during school hours. Programs such as "Sesame Street," "Readalong" and "Search for Science" are the products of this effort, and they demonstrate how effective the medium can be.

In the specific field of reading, there have been some extremely encouraging results from an experimental project conducted in Philadelphia. A high school English teacher there, Michael McAndrew, was searching for ways to improve basic skills and overcome his students' apathy toward reading. He hit on the idea of using television scripts to stimulate their interest. Starting with videotapes of some old commercial programs, the students were drawn into an involvement with the accompanying scripts. They responded immediately, and reading scores rose dramatically.

With the potential established, the next step was to seek advance scripts for programs not yet broadcast. The networks responded, and soon students were doing exercises with the scripts in anticipation of the scheduled broadcasts. They even took the scripts home, where they became the focus of family discussions.

The success of the project was vividly demonstrated with the broadcast of "Eleanor and Franklin," a remarkable two-part dramatization of the life of the Roosevelt family. IBM, the program's sponsor, agreed to print the script as an insertion in the *Philadelphia Inquirer* a few days before the first broadcast was scheduled. Additional copies were printed for all of the city's junior and senior high school students. Over a million scripts went out. Teachers and students worked with the scripts in advance, and on the appointed day "Eleanor and Franklin" drew ratings in Philadelphia of thirty-eight for part one and fifty-one for part two, compared with national ratings of twenty and twenty-four. The sense of participation had an immense effect. As an interesting sidelight, the Joseph Lash book on which the program was based sold out in the area, and libraries reported numerous requests for the book and others on the Roosevelts.

What this proves is that there is great potential for constructive use of commercial broadcasting as an educational tool. And the potential seems limited only by the imagination of educators and broadcasters. The networks are expanding their participation this year in the Television Reading Program, which grew out of the Philadelphia experiment. There is some evidence that the companion books growing out of television programs also are effective in attracting the interest of nonreaders. There are individual teachers making all kinds of uses of television, studying current events from news programs, reviewing dramatic shows, even examining the technology which makes television work. They are helped by the availability of the *Teachers Guides to Television,* a semiannual publication which provides lesson plans for fourteen television programs scheduled for the next semester. And, of course, at the college level, one can even attend class via television.

All of these developments are encouraging, and many of them involve books and reading for they are at the root of the educational process. I look forward to an expanded role for television as more educators take advantage of the potential it has for them and their students.

As I thought of the larger educational role of television in American society, I was drawn to a passage in John Platt's paper, which I mentioned earlier as a survey of education in an electronic age. He put it this way:

> Certainly television enlarges our world and links us more closely together. All human beings become parts of a simultaneous emotional response network. It is said that children in the first grade now know the meaning of many more words than children knew in 1900. How could they help it, after being exposed to all that diversity and life? Even adventure shows and old Westerns expand their horizons. And from age two to eighty-two, with TV debates and news, we have all learned about space, oceans, the environment, the limits to growth, energy, nuclear dangers, the antiwar movement, Watergate and the constitutional process, the Third World and hunger, women's liberation, and so on and on for dozens of major social and political issues that were not taught in disciplinary courses or in schools and colleges at all, until the students themselves insisted that they be brought into the classrooms.

That passage captures the great educational role not only of television but of all the mass communications media in a democratic society. Citizens must understand what is going on so they can understand what their leaders are saying. They must have knowledge in order to choose those leaders wisely. And they must be prepared to move in new directions when events or trends in the nation or the world dictate it. The timeliness of television is of special value in such cases.

The educational value of television was evident to all of us, I'm sure, during that unhappy summer of

1974 when we were changing presidents through the process of impeachment and resignation. That was a terribly critical time in the history of our republic, yet it went smoothly. Great credit must be given to the fact that people could watch the whole process, know what was happening and finally understand why the change must be made. They saw the House Judiciary Committee on their television screens day after day, becoming aware of the intelligence and good will of the members as they began the agonizing process of impeaching a president. They watched the president's rebuttals and finally his decision to leave. They saw a new president quickly and legitimately installed.

There were no destructive mysteries about the process, no room for dark suspicions of political plots. It was all there to be witnessed and thus provide the confidence that the political process had worked properly, guided by men and women of honor. It was crucial for people to learn all this and to learn it instantly so we could remain whole as a political family. Television was able to do that.

Now the role of the book has become manifest in the Watergate aftermath. We sometimes seem to be drowning in a flood of them, but in the long term they all will prove valuable for their contributions to our understanding of that tragic time. Books are bringing us the perspective and the detail, combined with a mosaic of the personalities and the diverse passions involved. In various ways, they will help us know why it all happened. Then they will store that knowledge to help future generations understand.

This contribution to understanding our political life is, of course, but one of the many roles of the book in our culture. Along with enlightenment, we depend on books for information, amusement, spiritual guidance, and myriad other benefits. But some kind of educational function is at the root of many of those roles, making an extraordinary contribution across a wide range of American life.

I am certain the Center for the Book is focused on the broader educational role of the book, for I have read and heard the comments of Dr. Daniel Boorstin and others guiding the Center through this formative period. I hope all of you who cherish the book will see that television has an equal, if somewhat different, responsibility to meet the diverse communication needs of our entire culture. And I hope you will see that the two are natural partners in informing and educating the American people.

Discussion

The first question from the audience concerned television programs such as Jacob Bronowski's "The Ascent of Man," a successful BBC television series that also was published as a book. Mortimer Adler was asked if this series was not an example of a television program that introduced viewers to "the pain of learning" and if, in fact, the series had not performed a useful function in producing a book? Dr. Adler pointed out that books such as *The Ascent of Man* are written without television and that he saw no reason to give television any particular credit for the volume. Furthermore, this program and similar BBC presentations, such as Kenneth Clark's "Civilisation," are really "the very extraordinary exceptions in the television fare." Finally, in comparing the television series and the book, he said that there was no doubt that the book demanded greater intellectual effort and provided greater opportunity for understanding, that is, for "turning back pages, comparing what is said on one page and on another." He concluded by reiterating: "the book requires something of the mind that television can never require."

Frank Stanton's comments on the topic highlighted his basic disagreement with Dr. Adler as well as his different approach to the entire question. He stressed, as in his earlier remarks, that books and television should be thought of as complementary means of communication, that we are not faced with "an either/or situation." He remarked that there were two secrets that always had fascinated him: the secret to the learning process and the secret to the motivational process. What television was doing vis-à-vis the book was motivating people to turn to books and "it could be used much more for that purpose than it is being used today in schools and in society generally." Jacob Bronowski's "The Ascent of Man," for example, introduced millions of people to new topics and ideas. Furthermore, Dr. Stanton reminded the audience, television is just one way to introduce people to books. Magazines and newspapers are others. For example, *Book Digest*, a new magazine with which he is associated, provides readers with excerpts from new books. The magazine has only been in existence for three years, but its circulation is now over a million, which, in his opinion indicates a strong and even a growing interest in books on the part of the general public.

The next question from the audience gave Mortimer Adler an opportunity to explain why he thinks liberal arts education in America has failed, a failure, according to Dr. Adler, that "started long before television came into its day." One reason is that the teaching of reading stops at the fourth grade "and most of our high school graduates are really readers at the fourth grade level." The teaching of reading and writing should go on for the whole of basic schooling.

He also underscored the difference in the ways he and Frank Stanton viewed the problem. He did not disagree with anything Dr. Stanton had said, for he did not think about books and television as means of communication and was not comparing them as such. Instead he was thinking about them in the learning process, and "television is a minor factor in the learning process if the learning process is to have anything to do with the cultivation of the mind." If the learning process is a method of developing the power to think critically and analytically, then "the ease with which television is watched has, I think, produced a kind of indisposition of the young and of our elders as well to make the kind of effort that good books require."

In response to another question from the audience, Dr. Adler expressed his doubt that television could ever develop to the point where group discussions could be held via television with the facility and immediacy with which they are held in person, as in adult Great Books classes, for example. It is true that closed circuit television presents opportunities for lectures and discussions between lecturer and student, but lectures, at their best, "are a poor second" to group discussions as an educational means. His favorite definition of a lecture is "a process whereby the notes of the lecturer become the notes of the student without passing through the minds of either."

The next questioner asked Dr. Stanton for his thoughts about the responsibility of commercial television for making television a more effective part of the educational process. The gentleman from the audience who posed the question said that it was essential for teachers to have external help if they were ever going to use television effectively. School budgets are decreasing, many teachers are prejudiced against or uninformed about television, and study guides or other printed materials that might supplement programs generally are unavailable. There are exceptions, of course, and one of them was the effort of NBC to disseminate information about "Holocaust" before the telecast. But in general there are many other programs and specials on commercial television for which there is no practical way for "meshing" television with the classroom.

Dr. Stanton began by saying that, while progress on the commercial side has been slow, the primary responsibility for educational programming lies with public television. Commercial television has a much broader audience than the one served by the classroom or public television. This does not mean that many of the programs on commercial television could not be used in the classroom, and some experiments along this line already are under way in Philadelphia and other cities. It is true, however, that commercial television has a long way to go, and there is no doubt that many viewers would learn much more from certain network programs if those programs were supplemented with printed materials. A joining of forces between broadcasters and educators is needed, for "too many times . . . educators have wasted taxpayers' money with equipment and production devices that yield little by way of product when they could work with local broadcasters and achieve better things on film than they could do alone." By the same token, "broadcasters should not try to be educators." They should "work with the educational system in using the medium of broadcasting more effectively."

The final questions from the audience dealt with the problems of adapting books for films, the selection and relevance of the books that are chosen for presentation on television (and the impossibility of adapting the best of books for film), the effect of television presentation on book sales, and the ability of television to move prodigious amounts of information around the world with incomparable speed. Dr. Stanton voiced his hope that someday we could find ways not only to use television more effectively but also to interest the television audience in serious books—the kind of books Dr. Adler had been discussing. In the meantime, however, we must accept television. It is here, it has changed our world, and "we have to find a way to use it effectively for education."

Ernest L. Boyer concluded the evening's discussion. He began by observing that the "distinction between information and education is a marvelous point to reflect on," and then directed his comments to "the process by which symbols are received." He said that a fascinating proposition about the conveyance of messages seemed to be coming from the evening's discussion. If the message "is formulated orally and received auditorally," it inherently presents "a less powerful education circumstance" than if it were put in print and received visually. The commissioner asserted that this proposition did not reflect the true nature of the problem. Instead, the question of whether a message is going to be useful educationally "has to do with whether the message itself is a significant message and whether the conditions upon its receiving provide for critique and reflection." Perhaps the most crucial point, he went on, was whether you receive a message in a circumstance which asks you "to formulate messages of your own."

The major problem with television, he continued, was its passivity—but one should not forget that this is often a problem with books as well, especially when readers have not been stimulated by a Mortimer Adler at an Aspen seminar. His worry is about "a generation that is not only receiving messages, but has never been asked to send messages, because in formulating messages to send one is required to think clearly, to organize, to sort out important from unimportant issues." "As I look at what is happening in the schools," he said, "we have developed through television in part a remarkable capacity to receive massive amounts of information . . . but considerable incoherence in formulating and sending messages, whether orally or in writing. And in the absence of that circuitry of message sending I think we have developed or can develop a generation where thought processes are diminished." Commissioner Boyer concluded by suggesting that possibly "both the book and television are diminished and limited unless they are enhanced by conditions in which messages are also to be reflected upon and messages formulated by the students in the form of seminars and discussion."

APRIL 27

THE VIEW FROM THE
WORLD OF COMMERCIAL TELEVISION

ROY DANISH

I had originally thought we might turn the seminar topic around and ask what the book can do for television, but I think you all know the book does a great deal for television. It provides us with materials which we adapt, sometimes cripplingly, sometimes magnificently, for television viewing.

The question, I think, has been put as precisely as it can be. How can we encourage reading, which is a central tool for our civilization, and what can we do to avoid the risk that the rewards which reading brings will be denied to a generation which has so warmly embraced another medium?

The prospect is not quite so scary as the question may imply. Young people are learning to read. They do read. But there are storm signals which seem to tell us that in a society which demands more skills of comprehension we have not learned to foster more desire to acquire and to use those skills.

I don't subscribe to the notion that this was once a nation of readers and is no longer so. Yesterday, like today, had its addictive readers. But as every book publisher and book seller knows, the avid book reader has never constituted a large part of the population, nor has our society placed a high value on readership. Bookworm has never been a word of praise. Bookish is not much better. And what about book learnin' compared with plain old common sense?

This is a land of action and hustle. The notion of a professional athlete wearing glasses is one that has only recently become acceptable. And his specs better look like an aviator's sunglasses.

Now, with that said, I'll try to get to the task that's been assigned me, and that is to describe the commercial television system, and it was even suggested that I defend it. Well, I'll offer you a brief description and no defense.

You've heard the statistics that describe television. All but two percent of our families have sets. Those sets are in use, depending on the season, between six and seven hours a day. Kids watch twenty-three, twenty-four, twenty-five hours a week; housewives, thirty; adult men a little less; teenagers, least of all; they're busy doing more important things. But more folks have television sets than have indoor plumbing or have telephones, certainly than have easy access to a library or book store.

Television is no longer as it once was, the universal family center. Now that nearly half our homes have more than one television set, viewing has become a more personal activity. And this does to some extent decrease the tension that develops on a windy fall afternoon when mother doesn't want to watch football. She has an alternative.

Almost all the statistics which describe television describe growth: number of sets, hours of use, expenditures by the public for their television sets, the money paid by advertisers, the money paid to program producers and creative talent. These have risen steadily and at a pace well ahead of the plaguing inflation.

Many of you know a great deal about television, both from your own perspectives and in the more general sense that anyone who's interested in the media will have observed the most salient features of this, the newest and the most pervasive. It's not news to you that the attraction which television programs hold for Americans provides the underpinning for a host of commercial enterprises. Many of these are in active competition with each other. The three major program sources, the national networks, compete fiercely, although they are alleged to be an oligarchy.

Similarly competitive are the television stations which serve individual communities. Program producers, both those who supply their products to the networks and those who launch them in syndication, compete vigorously.

And for all of these, the risks are considerable because the cost of developing programs is very high and the failure rate is crushing. Thousands of ideas, hundreds of story outlines are reviewed, and of the fifty or sixty pilots which actually go into production for a network each year the likelihood is that no more than two or three of these half-million dollar trial efforts will end up as even a modest success in a network schedule.

It sounds like a wasteful process; it is a wasteful process. And it tends to dampen the ardor of networks and stations and program producers themselves for the new and the untried.

On the other hand, producers, writers, directors, and performers are very understandably unwilling to gamble their time and their facilities for less than the going rate. There are no little leagues or off-off-broadway playhouses that serve as economical way stations for ideas and for talents. Whatever emerges from the developmental process must go into full competition with the most popular programming being shown to national audiences.

The costs of the entire enterprise—this comes as no surprise to you—are borne by advertisers. They foot the bills directly or indirectly for every program broadcast. I need not dwell on their purposes, which are quite simply to sell products and services. All but a very small number scatter their commercials through several programs because the cost of sponsoring individual programs is simply too high. And if an advertiser concentrates his advertising in a single program, he sacrifices the opportunity to reach toward those viewers who for one reason or another are not watching television at the time his broadcast is made or who have chosen to watch something else instead. It's for this reason that whatever influence advertisers exert over programming is in the form of a veto rather than in some more direct manner.

To the extent that advertisers as a whole find one or another sort of programming uncongenial for their advertising messages, those kinds of programs will be seen more rarely than others. Simply put, advertisers do not wish to associate their sales messages with programs which may give offense to substantial numbers of viewers.

Obviously, however, advertisers and broadcasters have not been persuaded that the television schedule should consist primarily of homilies, gardening tips, gentle children's stories, and good news.

Despite the complaints of pressure groups of various sorts, there will continue to be programs with violent action when that action is inherent to the plot. There will be programs with sex-related humor. There will be drama and comedy that explore many aspects of sexuality. There will be programs, comedic and others, that deal with sensitive moral issues. And there's room for all of these without sacrificing the diversity that leaves viewers free to choose among alternatives.

During most but by no means all hours of the day, broadcasters seek large audiences. They do this by offering what is approvingly regarded as popular by those who like it and who watch it and is derisively called popular by those who would prefer something else. It is quite patently a mixed bag. Within the span of a typical day the viewer can find news, soap operas, game shows, situation comedies, discussion programs, host shows, action and adventure stories, drama, feature films, music, an episode of a miniseries, and, on weekends particularly, a heavy schedule of sports. Not all of these program types are equally popular, as you can quickly learn by looking at the audience ratings.

It comes to us with a note of sadness that if you were to check the evening news ratings in major cities where there are stations not affiliated with networks, you'd find that a station's news program probably gets a lower rating than an off-network rerun. I don't know whether that's a comment on the quality of the news offered or on the desires of the audience.

This is predictably true also for many other highly respectable efforts, including religious and public affairs programs and those that you and I might agree present high culture.

Broadcasters accept as a given that the success of their enterprises depends to a large extent on the general level of approval which they enjoy in the communities they serve. And there's no doubt that approval stems in significant measure from the attention they give to the community's needs by providing programming which is relevant to them. News, public affairs, and certain other types of programs are a necessary part of that mix.

Today local news programs are popular enough to generate the advertising support it takes to make them profitable, although not as profitable as entertainment. The total cost of network news operations is still in excess of the revenues they generate.

Thus far I've offered you a fairly dry bone account of commercial television. Obviously, however, as your own viewing experience has shown you, much that is exceptional can be found imbedded in the typical daily matrix. While there's less risk taking than some would like to see, I can assure you that undertakings like "Roots" or the "Holocaust" or "60 Minutes" were not launched with any assurance of success. As it turned out, these have attracted very large audiences. Many other programs on which equally high store was placed have, by almost any workaday standard, been failures from the point of view of audience appeal. A recent disheartening example is "King."

The television audience does not respond to a

truant officer, and one must accept that Dr. Kissinger, despite his position as a world figure, can command only a tiny fraction of the audience which Henry Winkler assembles every week for "Happy Days." Nevertheless, Dr. Kissinger will be seen on the air again, if not quite as frequently as his namesake.

Now, what does all this mean to us here? Broadcasters think of themselves only incidentally as educators, and educators think of television broadcasting only incidentally as an adjunct to the instructional apparatus. But does that need to be the case? We in the broadcast industry do not think so. What's more, we've been attempting to develop bridges between the business we are in and the business of teaching.

Let me touch on a few of the activities which relate directly to the classroom and to reading. For many years broadcasters have provided, sometimes with advertiser support, sometimes without it, study guides for individual programs. For nearly ten years we have encouraged the publication and distribution of the *Teachers Guides to Television*, which appears each semester and has wide application for teachers of literature, the humanities, social studies, and other disciplines. With their lists of recommended books to be read, these guides are widely applauded, particularly at the top of the educational pyramid. But I'm sorry to report that as one works down toward the level of the classroom teacher we have found that traditional curriculums are not easily modified and old teaching habits die hard.

Some seventeen years ago my own organization funded the writing and distribution of *Television and the Teaching of English*, a book prepared by and for the National Council of Teachers of English. We did similar work with the National Council for the Social Studies. I was promised in those years that it would be a long time before such work would have any impact, and those promises came true. It's been a slow process. There are signs, however, that we are approaching a breakthrough as educators come to recognize that young people must be taught the audiovisual counterpart of literacy in a world in which so much communication occurs through the medium of television.

Ingenious uses have been found for run-of-the-mill television programming to make it serve the needs of teachers of reading and writing. Dr. McAndrew, here with us this morning, developed a method for engaging the interest and heightening the motivation of hard-to-teach students by providing them with the scripts for programs before they were broadcast. From this has grown an ambitious program by CBS which is encouraging similar activities in cities around the country. Dr. McAndrew's work and experimentation are also being expanded under the auspices of Capital Cities Corporation, a communications complex, and the results are so promising—and I know we'll hear from Dr. McAndrew later—that I honestly believe that this means for encouraging reading may become universal in the not too distant future.

Now, every librarian and every book seller knows that television programs based on books sell those books. Dr. Stanton told you a good deal about that last night. *Roots, Eleanor and Franklin,* and *Rich Man, Poor Man* are superexamples. But the so-called tie-ins are big book business and they're very hot items for younger readers.

If you're familiar with Prof. Harlan Hamilton's study of seventh grade boys and girls, you know that he concluded that these tie-in books were effective in promoting interest in reading among pupils in a low socioeconomic group and among those with lower IQ's. And Hamilton urges teachers to recognize and use student interest in television to motivate instruction.

Today we're seeing more of this phenomenon—the book based on the television show or on the film. And who's to say if books which have their genesis in this new and curious union are less effective as means to encourage more reading than *Silas Marner,* or God save the mark, *The Ordeal of Richard Feverel.* I bear those scars still.

As Stephen Seward said in a recent article in the *Wilson Library Bulletin,* it's beginning to look as if *TV Guide* has become an essential selection tool this season for librarians who are concerned with public demand.

But TV tie-ins need not be related solely to popular fiction and novelizations of TV series. Just consider what is available to the teachers of the classics. Television, both commercial and public, has offered Tolstoi and Stevenson, Dickens and Richter and Henry James, Trollope and Melville, Zola and Wilde and Crane and Defoe, and the list stretches on and on. There have been dramas from Shakespeare and from Barry, from Shaw, O'Neill, Williams, Wilder, and Ibsen, and others, of course.

Each of these works and adaptations has provided a splendid opportunity for teachers to open young minds to the mysteries and the delights of reading. If people, young and old alike, seek out television-related books on their own, just imagine what could be accomplished if teachers added their weight to this effort.

But enough. It's time for planning action and, with the help of this great institution and the Office of Education, progress should be swifter. Thank you.

Discussion

Lester Asheim suggested that commercial television's need to seek a large audience was perhaps the major reason the networks played such a limited role in stimulating the reading of serious books. Even the audience of one million reached by "Rich Man, Poor Man," for example, was too small for serious network concern.

Dr. Adler agreed that "the kind of books that are truly educative are read by a very small portion of the population, in school or out" but questioned whether this is necessary. If liberal education were extended to the total school population and all children made capable of reading, the situation could change. He added a final point of clarification:

I do know that children come to us as containers of different sizes. We have the half-pint child and the pint child and the quart child and the gallon child and so on up. When I say equal treatment of all of them, I do not mean putting a gallon of substance into the half-pint container. But what we are doing now is taking the half-pint containers or the quart containers as compared to the two-quart and gallon containers and putting in different kinds of filling—or trying to get different kinds of filling into them. I think we must put cream into each—a half-pint of cream in the half-pint containers as well as a gallon of cream into the gallon containers. When I have said this to large audiences of teachers and students they smile at me and say 'Well, you know, Doctor, you have never been in a big city school. You don't know those small containers have very small openings at the top. And cream is a very thick substance and doesn't get through easily.' And my answer has always been 'Get a funnel.' What we have to invent are the funnels for getting cream into the small containers. And that is the job we have not begun to face yet.

William Singer said he knew of many teachers who would love to get out of the rigors of regular curricula and seek "the broadening experience that television can be if the right funnel is found," but those teachers need assistance. The next question therefore becomes "who is responsible for finding those funnels?" Is it the responsibility of the television industry? The educational establishment? Private commercial sponsors? Roy Danish said that the prerequisite of basic reading skills was being overlooked. Unless a child can read "you cannot get on to accomplish the funneling of cream into a cup regardless of its size." He argued that any device or method that helped children learn to read was useful, including "studying the scripts of *Wonder Woman* before the program is seen."

Peggy Charren disagreed with Roy Danish on the point of television as a means of teaching reading. Television certainly can lead children to books, but in her opinion its use in teaching reading skills is limited. She returned, however, to the point Mr. Danish made in his prepared remarks about the image of books and readers presented on television. Programming directed to children should be "much more careful of the stereotype of the learned person or the reader . . . it is rare to see the book held up as something attractive." A more conscientious effort in this regard on the part of television writers and producers "will do more to get the child to the book than a program that is directed to teach reading or to teach the reading of a particular book."

Ms. Charren agreed with others who pointed out that given the commercial nature of our television system we cannot expect every program to be of special interest to those who care about the needs of the young. But she felt that special care should be taken in producing programs based on well-known books. She compared two different network specials based on Mark Twain's *A Connecticut Yankee in King Arthur's Court*. The first, an animation called "A Connecticut Rabbit in King Arthur's Court," was poorly done and "did nothing to bring back to me the book or provide any kind of experience for my children." The second, a dramatization to be shown this coming season, is much more promising.

Robert Geller asked for reaction from the network representatives to an idea that had been suggested by others: a moratorium on competition during time periods when a superior program is being shown, for example, a Saul Bellow program or "a Melville done entertainingly with a sense of adventure and suspense." There was agreement that such moratoriums were quite unlikely, but others pointed out that technological developments such as videotape recorders are now increasing viewer opportunities. In the past the viewer had to make a choice; today programs can be taped for later viewing.

FCC Commissioner Abbott M. Washburn made two points. First, he questioned the assumption of Mortimer Adler and Peggy Charren that television could not be useful in teaching reading. Current research, in his view, points in the opposite direction: television is being used quite successfully in teaching reading to elementary school children. Second, with proper planning and preparation, commercial television programs can provide children with significant educational experiences. He cited the recent NBC telecast of "Holocaust," which was watched by nearly ten million students and teachers in classrooms across the country. Supplementary materials were provided to teachers well in advance of the telecast, perhaps the most significant being the six pages devoted to the program in the *Teachers Guides to Television*. "Holocaust," with help from teachers and supplementary reading materials, effectively brought American school-children face-to-face with an important and controversial issue.

James Squire directed the attention of the group to another question: what is it that children need to be taught and need to learn in order to evaluate, cope with, and respond to television more effectively? It appears that we know very little about media literacy. What is it that children really are taught? During the thirteen schooling years, the schools themselves have only approximately twelve thousand instructional hours, compared to the sixteen to twenty thousand hours available outside the school. Can media literacy be defined for teachers? If we can do so, "we can expect to see television play a much more central and basic role in supporting the educational process." Howard Hitchens supplemented Mr. Squire's comments, reporting that the term used in the formal educational structure is "visual" rather than "media" literacy and that there even is an International Visual Literacy Association. One paradigm used by this group is an analogy between print literacy and visual literacy. Complete curricula based on the idea of visual literacy have been developed at the elementary and secondary level in several places in this country.

THE RESPONSIBILITIES OF
PUBLIC TELEVISION

HENRY LOOMIS

To borrow a page from Mr. Adler's book—you notice I have used the right word—I would like to read the questions that I was asked to address myself to, which are slightly different from those of Mr. Adler. "What is the place of the book in the television society?" Well, that's as easy answer. But, how can television be used imaginatively and effectively in the learning process? I think that is really what we're trying to talk about here. And, what practical steps can be taken at the national level to integrate television, the book, and the printed word within the educational process?

It seems to me that in the discussion so far, each of us is describing the elephant from our particular point of view. And, therefore, we are talking past each other as much as we are talking to each other. And part of that is because we haven't really agreed on definitions. I think that what we're talking about, in the final analysis, is the effect of books and television and learning itself on individuals. Mr. Adler uses the word reading when I believe he means thinking. He says reading doesn't count unless it's hard. I think what he means is that thinking isn't thinking unless it's hard. Whether you happen to read it or whether you happen to talk it in a discussion or debate, it is thinking. Reading may be an efficient way to make you think, but that's a different issue.

We're talking about how to give the individual a better insight into life, into himself or herself, into others; the full development of the person's capabilities, a better knowledge of right and wrong, a better knowledge of true and false, and sort of a general outline of how to improve the human race.

Let's define what we mean by books and television and learning. By a book, I presume we mean the written word that is bound and is moderately permanent. We assume that it's available through self-selection, whereby the reader selects the book and has access to it more or less at choice. This is, of course, not true of a student in school where the teacher instructs that person to read a particular book at a particular time and have a book report ready by nine o'clock the next morning. But that's a special case.

There seems to be an idea that books are good, although we admit that some of them are not. As a youngster growing up, I was told I should be careful not to read what were then called penny dreadfuls. They were still books in the sense that they were printed and bound. And I suppose they correspond to television's "Laverne and Shirley" or something of that nature.

A book requires imagination. In many ways a book is similar to radio. One is visual and one is aural, but both require imagination. Listening to a book read, a short story read on the radio, requires just as much imagination as reading a novel.

The discussion so far assumes that television is broadcast only. We now have cassettes and will soon have discs. I think that in our discussions we should separate whether we're talking about broadcasting or whether we're talking about the use of television or movies on cassettes or discs or some other form. Television and the movie tend to be emotional because you see things and get more involved. I think a key point about broadcasting is that a program provides a national experience that one individual seldom has with a book. "Holocaust" on television was a national experience. Enough people saw it at the identical moment that when traveling to work on the bus the next day

62

or going to lunch with somebody many people were talking about the same thing. You have a national experience when you see a man walk on the moon. You have a national experience when the president tells you that we are having a confrontation with Russia about Cuba or whatever the case may be. A book cannot provide this type of experience.

By learning, I presume we mean a deeper, wiser, creative process. But this requires self-motivation, and as Frank Stanton said yesterday, he doesn't know how you get people motivated. I don't think anybody does. You don't know how you get yourself motivated. We can all remember individual cases where we became motivated, but that doesn't make for a general rule.

Learning requires facts, it requires experience, it requires conversation with others, not necessarily teachers, but with others. Reading, as I said, I think, means in the way we are talking, thinking. The discussion, as some have said before, about which is the more important is really not necessary. For example, you can get into a discussion about whether a spark plug is more necessary than the rear axle. What difference does it make? You need them both or you're not going to move. And what is more, you've got to realize that you need more than either the axle or the spark plug. You need the rest of the car. I think when you talk about television and books as if they were the only two things, that is a false premise, again, for the discussion.

When we go back and take a look at the "Model A," that we heard about from two of our speakers last night, the implication was that it was television that took us away from the "Model A." I think that is clearly not the case. I think perhaps it was the automobile as much as anything.

Another important thing was the farm revolution, which also, of course, meant that you had the rural population depleted and moving to the urban area. The migration of minorities, the breakdown of the family, and the homogeneous social and geographic location that you used to have, the loss of the "Wild West" and all the rest of that thesis. One, of course, of the major changes is more individual leisure, and we all remember the old saying about "idle hands" and we know who uses them.

Let's take a look at public television and radio. And I suggest again that this discussion should include radio. Commercial radio is really not what we're talking about. Public radio is what we are talking about. Public radio is about to become the only national radio. It does not now exist. It once existed. It will exist again. And with the satellite interconnection and with numerous channels, I think we will then have a national aural experience which is not now possible. We have seen some of it in the Panama Canal Treaty debates and the impact that they had, which is significant.

The difference between public television and public radio is that we are knowingly and deliberately aiming at special audiences. Our largest special audience is children. When it comes to the amount of air time and the amount of money spent, we seek quality and we do it with very little money, which is another difference.

Our special audiences sometimes are called elite. By that, if you mean self-selecting in small groups, then they are elite. We carry, for example, probably more opera or ballet, something of that nature, than the commercial stations. Does that mean that we are elite?

I remember a copy of a letter I saw, addressed to one of our stations, concerning a newspaper review. The reviewer had accused the station of being elite because it carried symphony programs and ballet and the opera and only catered to the rich and the affluent. And this letter began, "I'm 22 years old. I am female and unemployed. I've only finished high school. I deeply resent the assertion in the review that therefore I do not appreciate the finer things in life and that I

64

cannot appreciate the ballet, that I do not enjoy the symphony, et cetera." And I think that is a very valid point. We try to have programs that are the best of the ballet for those who want ballet, and we recognize that this is only a small percentage of the population.

These are tiny audiences compared to the audiences that commercial television gets every evening. But they are many, many fold larger than the audiences for similar kinds of intellectual or artistic activities anywhere else.

I think the discussion to date has been based really on past technology. We are on the threshold of an entirely new technology, and presumably this discussion should be mostly about the future and what we should be doing in the next five or ten years, rather than what we might have done in the last five or ten years.

The greatest problem with a broadcast is the tyranny of time, that the broadcast that you want to see is on at eight o'clock tonight. Whether you've finished dinner, or whether you're on the phone with an important client or with Aunt Susie, it's eight o'clock. And if you want to see that program, you've got to cut off Aunt Susie and go see it. That's a terrible tyranny. We seem to expect the teacher to willingly submit to this same tyranny when the local public television station is broadcasting third year math at ten o'clock in the morning. "Damn it, stop what you're doing; it's ten o'clock! It's time for third year math. I don't care what your schedule is. This is it." And even more so if you're tied to the commercial stations. The fact that they're doing "Eleanor and Franklin" Tuesday night at nine o'clock means that you have to juggle your whole schedule so that Tuesday night at nine is the appropriate time in your personal schedule to watch "Eleanor and Franklin."

I think rather than trying to bring Mohammed to the mountain, we ought to do the reverse. New technology will do the reverse. We will bring television and radio on cassette and disc to the user without the tyranny of time. We will then permit the user to have the same control over what he or she sees or hears, permit the user to view it again and again, to stop in the middle and go back, and even permit the viewer to have a library of cassettes. What is the difference between that and a library of books? We can then compare and find out.

Discussion

William S. Rubens referred back to Robert Geller's question about a possible moratorium on competition. While it is not practical in terms of programming costs for any network to "abdicate its attempt to reach its audience," it is possible and even healthy for the networks to engage in "opportunistic scheduling." For example, NBC thought the program "King" would attract a large audience on its own, so it was willing to put it up against very competitive shows. The network thought that "Holocaust" would not be able to sustain an audience on its own, so on the second night it was scheduled against baseball, which is not strongly competitive. This type of competition or opportunistic scheduling can work to the viewer's advantage, especially when a network decides to move aggressively toward new and live programming.

Carll Tucker chided the assembled group for failing to recognize "that books are in competition with television." Unless this reality is faced, he said, we are living in a "dream world." If we want to attract children to reading, they must be moved away from television, and what we need is a strategy for achieving this objective. Mr. Tucker recalled Commissioner Boyer's earlier comments about growing up in Ohio and noted that one of the reasons education seemed somewhat easier at that time was that Dr. Boyer "was more or less a captive audience and education was his only escape from the confines of that Ohio town." Today we are "the least captive audience in the history of the world in terms of intellect." We are faced with a multiplicity of options of which television is only one, but it is an "extraordinarily seductive" lure. Books and magazines are also part of this "smorgasbord" of options, but they do not appear to be major attractions.

Mr. Tucker agreed with Mortimer Adler's point that the only real learning and thinking can come after literacy and that television does not teach people to think. He then outlined his strategy for attracting children back to books:

You use television to make book reading attractive, and you bring presssure to bear on the responsible parties to produce the kind of television shows for children which will make book reading attractive and which will raise the level of literacy. In addition to doing that, [you] persuade major corporations, which are the Medicis of our modern age, to help underwrite [the effort], because it is good for their image and it distracts everybody from their excessive profits. . . . The strategy has to be to get people back to reading books by using the tools of contemporary life.

Librarian Boorstin inserted "two footnote questions about definition" for seminar participants to ponder: Mr. Danish referred to programs that had been prepared but had "failed." What do we mean by failure? On television it appears that failure is "the inability to attract a big enough mass audience to command advertising." Second, "what do we mean by book or by television?" He continued:

Is it a book when we seek a Connecticut Yankee among the rabbits, or is it like trying to tell somebody about a ballet? It seems to me it's important for us to remember that we're starting from the assumption there may be unique value both in the television experience and in the book, and to be concerned with the question of what is the uniqueness of the two experiences and whether when we try to combine them we may not be making hash.

In responding to the remarks of Roy Danish and Henry Loomis, Robert Sklar addressed the problem of consultation between the television community and educators about "what should go on television that is of use in the classroom." He was surprised that there was not greater reliance on the educational community. In fact, the assumption seemed to be that the schools "should follow the leadership of television and that our choices will be limited to the choices made by people in responsible positions either in commercial or in public television." In both types of television, those decisions are made largely by people who necessarily have corporate interests in mind.

Gene Mater responded to Dr. Sklar. He explained that CBS has used advisors from the educational community since 1972, even though their activity has been limited to children's programming and in large part advising about the injection of "pro-social values in certain types of programs." In response to a question, Mr. Mater noted that while the teaching of "pro-social values," e.g., do not lie, do not cheat, go to school, etc., was hardly the type of teaching Dr. Adler was discussing, many others find it of great importance. More recently, CBS brought together the superintendents of schools from fifty large cities to discuss cooperative projects. The result was an agreement with twenty-two of the school districts for a project based on the CBS special "The Defection of Simas Kudirka." Scripts were published in local newspapers and local businesses supported the effort, which was quite successful.

Edwin Cohen took the position that "commercial television does not have a responsibility for education." If education is to be well served, it cannot be served through the happenstance of commerical television and its exploitation "for what it was not intended to do in the first place." Steven H. Scheuer "disagreed profoundly" with Mr. Cohen and summarized a project with which he was involved that was designed to create a "new kind of learning resource" both for public and commercial television.

To Pam Warford, Dr. Adler's "funnel" metaphor

was troublesome insofar as it implied passivity "or the pitcher theory of a child as being a receptacle." She said there was much to be learned "from thinking of children and what they bring to both the book and to television in an active way." As James Squire had noted in his comments about visual literacy, children need to bring critical skills not only to books that they read but to television viewing as well. She described a pilot project at ABC through which children are invited to review network television programs. From the reviews she has seen thus far, she is convinced that "we sell short the capacity of children to evaluate in an active way what they see."

As a preface to Michael McAndrew's remarks, Commissioner Boyer made several comments about the serious obligation we face in finding ways for television and the classroom to become more effective partners. What needs to be confronted is the relationship between television or broadcasting and the formal institution called the school and the materials within that school called the curriculum. He continued:

> There is some advantage in asking whether television can in fact be useful in developing the skills of communication, and I mean by that teaching children the processes of reading, understanding symbolization as a procedure, both auditorially and visually, through linear type as well as through molecules bombarding the tympanic membrane. . . . The second question, in my view, would be to what extent can television relate to the curriculum in the classroom? That to me represents a kind of second order question: how do we anticipate what television is going to do if it is essentially unguided in relation to the curriculum? Or, as I heard one exchange, should in fact the school and its curriculum to some extent lead television programming?

BRIDGE-BUILDING AND
THE EXPLODING ART FORM

MICHAEL J. McANDREW

Bridge: Any structure used to afford convenient passage over any obstacle.

The bridge I allude to is being constructed through the combined efforts of the media of the printed word and television, and this bridge is being directed toward the world community.

The use of the word "bridge" is rather significant as we investigate it more closely—and if there is a major obstacle which we have an opportunity to overcome, it would be the great need we have to understand and to master these media that exert amazing influences on our lives.

Generally, television and the printed word are considered competitors. But, uniquely, today these two giants are becoming more keenly aware that in the most substantive area, i.e., serving the community, they can complement each other.

And by joining forces they can begin to have an impact—a *significant* impact—in helping to resolve some of the major obstacles that exist in the world: (a) by helping to eliminate illiteracy throughout the world, (b) by helping to develop a greater understanding and appreciation of our fellow human beings, (c) by helping to relieve apathy—indifference at levels that most affect our lives, (d) by helping to create an atmosphere for dialogue within the family, within the community, (e) by helping to support and to direct a renaissance in education, in the traditional classroom, as well as outside the classroom.

Bridges, indeed, are being built—and we all will be served better because of them.

The phenomenon of "Roots" has caused many people to research their origins, to take great pride in their varied cultural backgrounds.

Well, television's roots have been similarly researched and have been found to be firmly planted in the fertile ground of the printed word. Its excitement, its intrigue, its comedies, its series, its dramas, its documentaries, its news, its successes, and its failures all begin with the mastery of the printed word.

Television began for me some years ago when several men, dressed in service station uniforms, introduced themselves in song as the men from Texaco—and then gave way to a most dominant personality who immediately lit up the tiny screen and assumed the title of "Mr. Television." In those days, television borrowed quite liberally from all avenues—burlesque, vaudeville, radio, nightclubs, the stage, yes, even the classroom.

But slowly, methodically, through the efforts of artists such as Chayefsky, Serling, Rose, Gibson, Vidal, Costigan, Blinn, Kinoy, Brooks, Henry, Reiner, et al., television began to evolve a distinct art form of its own; one that established its parameters, recognizing its strengths, its weaknesses—one that writers, performers, artists of all kinds could come to grips with and grow with. And this art form began to capture the imaginations of an entire world.

This art form has brought about an unusual wedding between the ubiquitous electronic medium and the equally ubiquitous medium of print. And neither will ever be the same again.

With the aid of the major television networks and some major newspapers throughout our country, entire television scripts of worthwhile network specials have been published in advance of their being "aired" on television. With the aid and direction of local school systems and the cooperation of the newspapers involving the entire communities, these publications have met with overwhelming success and approval. It has caused a usually passive medium to become a challenging, active medium.

Programs such as "Jane Pittman," "Eleanor & Franklin," "Roots," "Missiles of October," "Defection of Simas Kudirka," "Everyone Rides a Carousel" have become integrated into language arts and/or social studies disciplines of major school systems wherever this cooperative venture has taken place. It has, at the same time, established unprecedented activities for home viewing, discussion, role playing, critical analysis.

With the aid of the major networks—allowing use of their most popular series' scripts, in advance of their being aired on network television, a major reading program has been developed using these scripts accompanied with appropriate teachers' guides which focus attention on comprehension, vocabulary, and writing skills.

These skills are based entirely on the context of the television script. This school year over sixty-five thousand students from grades 4-12 in four major sites —New York City, Washington, D.C., Philadelphia, and Montgomery County, Pennsylvania—have had programs such as "Waltons," "Little House On The Prairie," and "Happy Days" used supplementary to their existing reading programs. This program is being evaluated by Pennsylvania State University.

Preliminary attitudinal surveys have demonstrated outstanding success, revealing a more positive interest in reading, elimination of discipline problems, a marked increase in free reading, and an interaction at the home level among the parents, children, and older relatives that is most encouraging. Data relative to advancement in skills areas will be available sometime this fall. We are also using these scripts and teachers' guides in schools for the hearing-impaired and those classes with English as a second language with equally positive results.

Motivation seems to be the catalyst. People are being reintroduced to the excitement of the world of print. Inquiries have come from well over forty-two hundred school systems throughout our country, ranging from Los Angeles, Chicago, to a Navajo reservation. Inquiries have also come from Great Britain, Canada, France, and Mexico.

This one bridge carries with it so many opportunities—challenges that hopefully will be met within the classroom to take advantage of that motivation, that excitement, and channel it with proper direction so that the children can be introduced to a whole world of adventure and success; challenges that hopefully will also be met in the fields of print and television.

These challenges are great and awesome—for they will demand of the forces that are constructing those bridges better programs, better writing, more creative writing; for the world community is desirous of becoming more aware, more demanding, more constructively critical, more in command of their viewing and reading habits.

The exacting toll for crossing this bridge just may be the fulfillment of a better life for everyone.

WB
for
NSF
talk
2/8/79

(cf old Olivier Shakespeare movies, Henry V, Hamlet, etc

admin

get school superstructure
tuned in   so " unit plans "
etc. are   in tune with these
" pre-viewing " script-reading
opportunities !   wh 2/3/79.

Discussion

Mortimer Adler referred back to the phenomenon of the "Holocaust" telecast, with its hundred million viewers, and suggested that the program shed little light on *why* the holocaust happened or "what are the causes in human life and human society [that enable] so extraordinary an event to take place." Furthermore, it seemed unlikely that many of those who watched "Holocaust" would be able to read the two books that can shed light on it: Hannah Arendt's *The Origins of Totalitarianism* and Machiavelli's *The Prince*. Dr. Mc-Andrew responded that he was certain that "Holocaust" had provided an introduction to many viewers who would pursue the subject further and perhaps even read the two books recommended by Dr. Adler.

Robert Logan said that thus far seminar participants had not tackled the crucial topic of "how television affects people's thinking and how print affects people's thinking." He emphasized the importance of writing for our thinking processes, pointing out that when one learns to read, one doesn't learn just to decipher symbols—one learns how to think in an analytic fashion. He said that

> the big problem we're facing with television is that it's inundating our young people's minds and not giving them the opportunity to really come to grips with reading skills. . . . Through the easy access of information through television, we begin to lose those analytic skills which allow us to create more information. . . . We don't want to fill up those containers. What we really want to do with our children is to turn them into cows so they can create their own milk.

Brian Brightly directed attention toward "one of the last labor intensive marketplaces of the world—

teaching." He cited a recent study showing that 55–60 percent of U.S. teachers and principals favor the use of television in the classroom and about 33 percent of the teachers use instructional television at least one hour per week. One of the major problems in bridging the gap Dr. McAndrew discussed is in defining the role that each segment—teacher, commercial television, public television, federal government—should play, and he hoped this conference would be of assistance.

A pitfall in one bridge-building effort was described by Erik Barnouw. He recently visited a junior college that was making heavy use of video cassettes and films. The man showing him around the library, where there were rows and rows of students viewing cassettes instead of reading books, thought that the new audiovisual facility was most important, since "our reading level here is eighth grade." He was, in effect, saying what John Platt stated in his article, that "maybe we should bypass the problem of literacy and educate in this way." As he was guided around this "impressive" facility, Dr. Barnouw began

> to have a terrible feeling that eventually we would have an elite class of people who could cope with the printed page, who have access to the mysteries of the past and whose job it would be to produce docu-dramas, constantly reevaluating the past history for the present generation. For the older people there was only the present. Now this is a nightmare idea expressed in the book *1984* and we are very close to that stage if we don't look out. . . . We should not be ready to give up on literacy, as [John Platt's] article suggests, but address the problem of how we can save the book.

Karen Klass addressed Mortimer Adler's "despair with the state of the schools today." She noted that teachers and television share a common problem: parents who turn their children over to the teacher, in much the same way that they turn them over to the television set, and then blame the teachers and blame television for the child's attitudes, behavior, and values. She suggested further investigation of the matter of ultimate responsibility for the child's education and said that perhaps we should "look at how we would share this responsibility among the educational community, government, industry, and the public at large." In response and agreement Dr. Adler reiterated his position that if children are watching twenty-five hours of television a week, "it isn't television's fault. It's our fault if we yield to it." Moreover, "America is getting the kind of school system it deserves in terms of its values and its commitments. To make it better, the public demand must be better. The parents must be better."

William Rubens observed that as far as he could see, it was not the amount of television watched that was the problem. Current research shows no correlation between the amount of television watched and the amount of reading. In fact, children who watch a great deal of television also tend to be heavy "media consumers," doing more reading of both good and bad books, having more friends, and in general being more active and gregarious than most other children.

Grace Hechinger said that "if we say America has the kind of schools it deserves . . . we also have to say America has the kind of television it deserves," for television, like the schools, directly reflects our culture. She was unhappy, however, with placing *sole* blame for either situation on the schools, or on parents, or on television. In addition, she urged the group to consider what children *do* learn from television, which may be quite different from what people intend to teach them, a circumstance comparable to the one that often occurs in school. One of the most interesting reactions of children to "Holocaust" was their inability to believe it really happened "because they are not used to dealing with television in a way that is real to them."

In spite of Mrs. Hechinger's thoughts on the topic, Marcus Cohn placed the sole blame on parents, observing that most television viewing by children is done "without parental guidance or parental participation." Parents have abandoned their children to television. Television is passive and requires no analysis or thought. Reflecting on her experience as both a broadcasting executive and a mother of four children, Kathryn Broman agreed with Mr. Cohn regarding parental responsibility. Her two youngest children were "practically raised in a television studio" but they never were allowed to watch television until all their homework was finished, and even then "they were never abandoned to the television set." Other seminar participants discussed the importance of parents as role models: if parents watch a great deal of telvision, their children probably will do the same. If parents read, their children are inclined to be readers.

"Without cheating and moving my section of the program up to this part," Ann Kahn of the Parent Teachers Association added her comments. She agreed that parents had the primary responsibility but thought that the problem required "facing an enormous imbalance in the relative use of one area of learning as against another." For we now have the technical ability to develop portable television sets roughly the size of transistor radios which will soon enable children to watch television by themselves outside the home. Naturally they will watch "whatever they darn well please" and children watching television will no longer be under "this fantastic control of their parents that we seem to long for and which I think is not really realistic." We must face this imbalance not just as parents but as citizens.

William Singer described a survey of teachers that asked what subjects, as opposed to programs, were of special interest for the use of television in the classroom. Teachers seem to have a special interest in law enforcement, television itself, education and educational values, consumer topics, and economics. Singer's firm, Prime Time School Television, is developing curriculum units such as "Television and Economics: From the Medium to the Marketplace," in which there seems to be a great deal of interest. Such programs serve as bridge builders just as the *Teachers Guides to Television* provides assistance. Finally, Mr. Singer disagreed with Marcus Cohn's opinion that people did not discuss what they saw on television. There are many instances when television can be a terribly exciting stimulus for discussion. "Holocaust," of course, is the most recent example. The program provoked widespread controversy and discussion, most notably through the newspaper comments of Elie Wiesel and Fred Friendly.

The notion of bridge building was viewed from a "slightly different perspective" by Howard Hitchens. He explained that within the educational establishment there are a large number of people who work at bridge building "by viewing the book as printed material and television as an electronic communication medium for the purposes of improving instruction." This is a different approach from the one being taken in this seminar, which he felt viewed "book" primarily from a publisher's perspective and "television" from the standpoint of the commercial broadcasting business.

Ernest L. Boyer concluded the morning session with comments on several of the points raised during the discussion. He began by reinforcing Mr. Tucker's remarks about the relationship between "captive audiences" and education, especially the importance of extending the worlds of information in order to stimulate thought. Today television, magazines, radio, and paperbacks have extended the worlds of our children in ways that are difficult for older generations to perceive. The formal school structure must redefine itself within this new context of multiple sources. To put it another way, there now are "many classrooms" and "many teachers" and this is a fundamental change that educators must face. The commissioner felt one way of gaining an insight is to question the children, the students themselves, and it seemed to him that in one instance

> they view the traditional structures, the ones we prize, with less reverence, more suspicion, sometimes open scorn, [and they are] quite more willing to challenge the traditional sources of authority because they early on have themselves acquired alternate sources of knowledge which they feel they can pit against the classroom, and perhaps even the book.

The ground rules of the classroom have changed, for the student now has a new capacity to challenge the teacher, to state, "That's not the way it is," sometimes adding the footnote "because of what I saw on television."

Dr. Boyer stated his view that there are ways by which television can enhance basic classroom skills, but he was unsure if television could assist beyond that almost mechanistic function. He was, however, struck by Dr. Logan's comments about the importance of the relationship between written symbols and thought processes. Since there is a relationship between expanding vocabulary and the capacity to expand one's ability to think, maybe it is true, as some have asserted, that television can only take us to a certain plateau of thought because written symbols are needed to take us further. This led the commissioner to pose two final questions to the seminar participants:

> What . . . are the prospects of expanding knowledge through television and what are its limits? And at what point are written symbols in fact the building blocks of knowledge?

He concluded with the observation that understanding what television can and cannot do to move students in the formal classroom is an intriguing kind of theoretical question which we probably will be exploring for some time.

80

THE VIEW FROM
THE WORLD OF PUBLISHING

DAN LACY

After having heard with great interest the remarks of Frank Stanton, whose former company, CBS,
is one of the world's great book publishers, and of the
many people from NBC, whose parent company, RCA,
through its ownership of Random House and Pantheon,
is perhaps the country's distinquished literary publisher, I'm glad, as a representative of a proprietor of
a group of TV stations, to have the opportunity to say
something this afternoon. I feel sometimes I've fallen
into a sort of autumnal and skeptical stage of life, and
I'm inclined to suspect that almost every generally accepted belief is probably not true, and particularly generally accepted beliefs that are passionately held, and
I think the discussion of books and reading and television is particularly obscured by some of these.

One of them is the belief that somehow television
is obliterating reading as an art. Mr. Stanton last night
gave some very interesting statistics on the tremendous
increase in the sale and distribution of books and the
library circulation of books during the television era.
I can add to that only that the per capita sale of books
(in copies, not dollars) in the United States today is
probably about three times what it was twenty-five
years ago at the dawn of the television era. And this
isn't entirely mass market paperbacks by any means.
The university press output is perhaps ten times what
it was twenty-five years ago. The number of serious
scholarly journals has all but exploded.

When you consider the enormous shift in the
makeup of the work force, from unskilled jobs not re-

quiring the use of reading to skilled and professional jobs which require extensive reading both in preparation and in the daily conduct of the job, I think there's no question at all that never before in history have people in this or any other country spent so many hours a week reading, whether books, magazines, newspapers, or memoranda, as they do now.

The second belief is the one I think set forth quite eloquently in the romantic paper by Mr. Platt distributed in advance, which suggests that television, particularly when cable and discs are added, is going to open up an enormous flood of exciting and enriching materials that will revolutionize the whole conduct of education. He's really not talking about broadcasting. He's talking essentially about the use in classrooms of tapes and discs which don't really differ from the educational films that have been available to us for a generation, except that they give us a somewhat poorer image, and they demand less mechanical skill on the part of teachers to use them.

I think our experience with the great revolution that was going to happen with educational films suggests that classroom use of these materials will be useful and desirable and will increase at a moderate rate, but that it will not in any revolutionary or drastic sense alter the patterns of education.

I think the third myth is the old gray mare syndrome, the belief that somehow there once existed a Camelot in the United States in which hot dogs, apple pie, books, and Model A's went together to symbolize the American life, and all American children sat around all evening reading books.

Obviously, the old gray mare never was what she used to be. Very few people ever read many books in this or any other country, and I think a source of delusion is that many of us who think a lot about these things grew up in book-oriented homes and had book-oriented childhoods, and, hence, tend to project our own childhood experiences back in the recollection of that era. I think this is certainly true of a lot of what we perceive as a dramatic new problem of marginal literacy, or illiteracy, in the core city populations of our country. We forget that this marginal literacy or illiteracy was there all along. It was just invisible on the plantations in Mississippi or Puerto Rico, and it's become very visible when you moved it up to a large city and into occupations where reading became a necessary function.

Now, does all this mean that we aren't really talking about anything very important? If books aren't dying and television's not going to enter the classroom in ways that provide a revolutionary transformation of education, and if there never was a paradise from which we've been cast out, are we saying that none of this matters very much? Not at all. I think there are two or three very important ways in which written matter, printed matter, printed words, differ from other media of communication and experience and that these differences and their relative social roles have great importance.

I'd like to express this by reading a part of an article of some years ago on words:

"Words, written words, relate us to life in ways quite different from the flow of sound and image or from the austere numerics of the computer. They are not different ways of doing the same thing: they are ways of doing different things. The uniqueness of words is that they are all abstractions, and yet all are metaphors. No word, no flow of words embodies life whole. Each reaches into the swirl of life and extracts some one characteristic to name. To say that a man is 'tall' or 'blonde' or 'generous' or 'cowardly' is to say one thing of an infinity that might be said. Whatever we say of the simplest event is only the tiniest part of the whole truth and is stained with the falsity of incompleteness. Abstractness is double the character of written words. Spoken words are themselves a part of the event; they act as well as describe, but the written word pulls its little fragment of meaning from the flowing whole of the universe and removes it in space and time remote from the reality to which it relates. The words with which we write of any part of human experience omit most of the reality and separate us from the little they single out. And it is this abstractness, this remoteness cutting us off from life, that makes the printed word unsatisfying to those who seek an immediacy with the whole of life. Film and television and stereo sets and transistor radios provide a flow of communication that can be sensed directly, without the intervention of comment or description—in a wordless, quite literally, in an ineffable communion. . . . But it is this very abstractedness and remoteness that make words the instruments of power. Bathed in life one can only feel it, not understand or master it. Only with the word-given power of abstraction does it become possible to perceive the twoness of all pairs, the blueness of all blue things, the coldness of all cold. Words are like the tongs by which a scientist, safely beyond lead walls, reaches into the fatal radiance of an atomic pile, pulls out what he wants for examination, manipulates it, lays it side-by-side with another bit. It is a magical power. Words not only bear meaning: they create it. Truth itself is a kind of relation between words and reality, a relation that did not exist before words. All science, all mathematics, all technology above the primitive, all philosophy, are the product of words. They are the instruments to master the ambient universe, whether in the simplest sense of technology or in the higher sense of comprehension. They are the instruments of transcendence of time and place, the means of forming universalities stretching through time and across space."*

I think perhaps we don't realize that there was only a relatively brief period in our history when print

* Dan Lacy, "Words, Words, Words," *Arts in Society* (Madison: University of Wisconsin, 1972), pp. 300-303.

really dominated mass life. From the early sixteenth century until roughly the end of the nineteenth century, print was the only means of vicarious experience we had. Travel was difficult. There were no motion pictures. There was no radio. It was almost impossible even to print a photograph. Until photographs came, we had only woodcuts and etchings. There was a great poverty of vicarious experience, other than in this form of print where experience had been abstracted, organized, arranged in linear process. We were almost compelled to see the world in those ways.

And only in the latter half of the nineteenth century did this access to print become a really mass availability. Until the mid-nineteenth century the fact that printing presses were hand-operated, the paper handmade from rags alone, very severely limited the access to print.

By the latter half of the century—with a steam powered press, mechanical paper, the telegraph that could disseminate news, and the rail system that could carry magazines and books rapidly across the country —for the first time you had a print-oriented society, and that persisted even to my boyhood. I grew up in a home without radio, without sound motion pictures, without color reproductions of works of art, without anything but scratchy, three-minute recordings of individual arias for music. And we've had our whole ability to realize life transformed into a different sense in which we are able to spend a great deal of our time in the reception rather than the organization of ideas, not only through broadcasting but through films and through recorded music and through a variety of other devices.

There was a period in the 1960s when we felt that most of our economic problems were solved and that what we needed to do was to get out of the productive rat-race and devote ourselves to more sensitized communion with life. This was the mood of college students who evaded courses on engineering to take courses in Zen Buddhism and art appreciation. There was a denigration of reading as a painful discipline to organize and control life, contrasted with the disciplines that simply experienced and enjoyed it.

As we come into the late 1970s and realize that things are tough all over and are going to get tougher —that with the energy shortage and the other production difficulties and with jobs declining and unemployment—the ability to organize life, to master it, to deal with it, to work with it assumes a new importance. We have had concomitantly an emphasis on a return to basics in education, a restoration of attention to these disciplines that abstract and organize experience in ways that make it possible to manipulate and master it, not merely to sense it.

I think it would be a great tragedy to our life if the ability to read, both in the narrower sense and in the broader sense that Mr. Adler referred to, were lost or diminished. And one is given some concern by the declining scores on reading tests and such things as college entrance boards and achievement tests given, which have been widely attributed to the preoccupation of children with television. Maybe this is so, though it's difficult to tell. My own guess would be that it's the other factor that Mr. Adler mentioned, that we are continuing the education of a much larger mass of children through much longer periods of time, and I would also guess that, however, it's a problem of the schools themselves.

I remember hearing once an assistant commissioner of education, who later left to become a superintendent of a large city school system, saying, essentially, some people learn through reading, others learn better audiovisually. Why do we have this elitist concept that everybody's got to read? Why don't we take those for whom reading isn't comfortable, recognize them as of equal dignity, and teach them with films? He thought of this as a racially egalitarian attitude because it was really black students he was talking about, though he didn't use the word. And what he was saying in effect was that it isn't worth teaching blacks to read. Let them grow up without the ability and if they can't get a job as a delivery boy because they can't read street addresses, that's just too bad. It was one of the most contemptuous attitudes I've ever heard.

I think the schools, faced with a difficult set of student bodies, have too often resigned themselves to saying let's make the curriculum easy so that the less gifted or less privileged or disadvantaged student can cope with it, rather than going into the tremendous extra effort to create a uniform level of reading ability regardless of background.

The other area that does give me some concern is the new communications technology of the twentieth century, which has increased the ability of one or a very few communicators to reach a very large number of people, so that one president can speak and be heard by seventy million people, say, on television. Almost the only part of our communications system that works in the opposite direction is books, and particularly books organized in collections in libraries which bring together for one reader tens of thousands of authors rather than for one speaker audiences of tens of millions. And I think creating in our society systems that sustain this ability of individuals to control their own access to communication is a tremendously important thing.

There's been a decided diminution over the 1970s of the intense interest that had developed in the 1960s for public support of libraries at all levels in this country, including school libraries, and in general the support of all media of communication and instruction in the schools, so that today less than 1 percent of our school budgets over the country as a whole go for any kind of educational material, textbooks, library books, films or anything else. If we're really talking about dealing with any of these problems, whether it's using television intelligently in the schools or whether it's sustaining an attention to reading and books, I think a first step is simply facing up to the fact that we've not made the commitment of educational appropriations. A shift of half a percent from other expenditures to materials would equip schools to effectively use audio and audiovisual materials as well as books in their work.

Discussion

Dr. Boorstin asked Margaret McNamara to comment on Mr. Lacy's remarks and to describe the role and function of Reading is Fundamental, Inc. (RIF), of which she is founder and chairman. Mrs. McNamara explained that RIF was established to breach a gap that publishers, schools, and libraries have difficulty filling —getting books into the hands of children. With the cooperation of publishers and, especially, local groups around the country, RIF *gives* paperbound books to children. She outlined how RIF functions, emphasizing the importance of freedom of choice in selecting titles, book ownership, parental involvement, community support, and close cooperation with libraries and schools, and said that putting books in the hands and homes of children was a vital form of bridge building.

The Librarian next asked Cyril Busbee to make any observations he would like from his perspective as a state superintendent of education. Dr. Busbee described the commitment the state of South Carolina has made to educational television, pointing out that "over two-thirds of our schools and school children regularly utilize the educational TV programs which are broadcast as a state enterprise by the State of South Carolina." He also outlined how the educational television system is used by the schools and the difficulties encountered in "getting the educational community to accept TV." Especially resistant are those teachers who know their classroom performances cannot compete with the television presentations. One of his greatest concerns, however, is the copyright situation. The schools themselves now have the capability of "recording and taping and replaying programs of educational value and merit," but when it is legal and when is it illegal?

Dr. Boorstin provided seminar participants with two reminders. Several persons had commented about "fear" of television on the part of teachers; we should not forget that "only a few hundred years ago their ancestors were fearing the book." Secondly, with reference to the copyright situation, the Copyright Office of the United States is part of the Library of Congress. On Capitol Hill one of the things we discover is that "laws not only can be made but they can be changed, and one of the purposes of this meeting and of future meetings of this group of the Center for the Book is to discover how the laws of the United States can and should be changed to suit the purposes of our collaboration."

Mortimer Adler accented several points made by Dan Lacy. He stressed the importance of the word, in linear form, as the "indispensable instrument for dealing with abstractions" and added that "the organization, management, and creative use of abstractions is the highest form of human learning and the most important part of our civilization." Television, or films, or any other media "will always be inferior to the use of words" and especially to "an extended discourse on the printed page." In conclusion, he noted that "what distinguishes man from other animals is conceptual as opposed to perceptual thought" and "the kind of thinking that goes on when you watch a television series is perceptual thinking, not conceptual thinking." Perceptual thought, of course, is part of human life and "is not to be despised," but it is "by no means the highest form of thinking or the most important form or the most useful form in terms of controlling our society or our lives."

Dr. Boorstin next called on Martin Kaplan, executive assistant to the Commissioner of Education, to make an announcement. After explaining that "one of the happy things about this meeting is that it is the beginning of a collaborative effort between the Library of Congress and the Office of Education," Dr. Kaplan announced that the Office of Education would soon issue, under the auspices of the Special Projects Act, a request for a proposal for competitive bids for "the development, production, dissemination, and utilization of radio and television programming for educational purposes in the home and the classroom." He explained that:

> The purpose of the request for a proposal will be to link television and radio, the classroom, and the home toward the purpose of learning, and happily this discussion today has helped us to define and refine our approach to that set of goals. We hope that the applicants for this proposal . . . will devise ways to use existing television and radio programming, both public and nonpublic, to teach the basic skills, the fundamental tools of learning. . . . A second goal is to stimulate an interest in books. That set of goals, that subset rather, includes books not only as entertainment but also as sources of information and understanding. . . . Finally, the purpose of the proposal will be to move our audiences, children and parents alike, from being the passive recipients of information to the active participants in what goes on in television and radio programming, and ideally active participants in the world of books and learning as well, a movement from being the receptacles, the jars that one merely fills, to those who exercise their critical skills both in terms of the television and radio programming that they are receiving and also in terms of the text to which we hope they will turn.

The subject of copyright was discussed. Henry Loomis stated that the clarification of the copyright law in the broadcasting area was probably "the single most important" improvement that could be made on the national level. In his view "we have to develop, as we have in the publishing business, a copyright system and a scale of fees that makes economic sense for not only the author but also for the distributor." Dr. Boorstin and Ivan Bender of the Copyright Office responded. Mr. Bender summarized the status of current efforts in the Copyright Office to clarify the issue and promised to see that the concern of Mr. Loomis and other seminar participants about its urgency was transmitted to Barbara Ringer, the register of copyrights, and others who are working toward a solution.

TELEVISION
MADE FOR THE CLASSROOM

EDWIN G. COHEN

I would like to begin by distinguishing television made for the classroom from the other kinds of television that have been talked about up to this point. The programming that is originated and delivered through commercial television, is seldom, if ever, made for the classroom. It has value through adaptation and that's the kind of capitalization, exploitation, that we have been talking about. It is a great resource that should be extended in terms of its utility.

Public broadcasting at the national level does not yet create program material that is made for the classroom. Most of the television that is used in the classroom is delivered by the broadcasts of individual non-commercial television stations, public television stations. They are the distributors typically of school programming. At the national level the interconnected public television service does not design and deliver programs made for the classroom.

In the few minutes that we have here, I would like to take you on a quick tour of the secret world of school television that has not been visited yet, I believe. What is it we're talking about? What does it look like?

Typically, what we're talking about are series of television programs that are designed for weekly use in the schools, either over the whole of the school year, thirty consecutive weeks, or for one semester, fifteen consecutive weeks. Typically, these programs are used by elementary school teachers as part of the regular classroom instruction provided by them. Each program is generally fifteen minutes in length and is conceived and utilized as part of a longer lesson which may extend the total time, including the television transmission, to thirty or forty-five minutes spent on the theme that is initiated by the television program.

The crucial point is that television made for the classroom is intended for instruction. It is not accidental; it is not incidental. The material in terms of its topic is chosen because it is relevant to what the schools are trying to do. It is relevant to the curriculum. It is designed to be best used with particular boys and girls in terms of their ages, in terms of their grade level. It is typically designed in length not to exceed the total time that is available for instruction in a given area. A ninety minute program in music, no matter how beguiling or useful it might be in the eyes of some, exceeds by two the total amount of time that is typically spent in music instruction during a whole week in American schools right now.

The program is not designed to stand on its own. It has to have additional activity between the people in the class under the management of the teacher. As a consequence, a fifteen minute length seems about right when you want to have the teacher devote thirty or forty-five minutes in addition to the time of the television program.

The material has to be somewhat efficient in the sense that you can't beat around the bush and suggest that this is the content. You've got to come right out and say it. You've got to pack as much content as you can within these fifteen minutes. It is a question of density. It is the difference between voluntary light reading density and the textbook, if you will. And crucially, the school television program is organized for learning (to the extent that we know about what that means).

The characteristics of these materials in an instructional sense are that they can serve a variety of instructional purposes, sometimes more one than the other but generally all three of the major notions: that you have got to motivate the learner, you have to expose some content, and you have to provide an opportunity through application for learning.

We've seen a number of tapes of children in the classroom. We know that they watch the screen showing a well-designed television program. We don't know whether they're involved or whether they're passive when they're watching the screen, but that's the primary test that school television programs have to meet.

There are a number of devices that are used increasingly to involve the viewers actively during the course of the program. Because school television may seem mysterious, let me call to mind the National Drivers' Test, where the audience as in the old Pete Smith shorts at the movies, is actually quizzed during the course of the program. This is a kind of an involvement. There are more sophisticated involvements such as a read-along series, where the youngsters are actually—and I won't get into a debate or anything about the meaning of the word—but the youngsters are helped to master the skills of reading by shouting out, by raising their hands, by predicting in advance what's going to happen, not just to keep them awake but because it is the involved viewer that becomes the best learner.

Crucially, the television program is integrated with other learning activities and materials. It is a dirty trick, but most television programs that are used in the classroom force activity afterwards that the teacher must manage. If the teacher is uncomfortable with managing activity because he or she is not prepared or feels it is irrelevant, the teacher has the option of either turning off the set or, crucially, never using that series again. This is the characteristic that I think lies at the heart of school television, that it is entirely voluntary on the part of the teacher to use or not to use, to repeat the use year after year or not to repeat.

I stick my neck way out here, but I would say not

only that television is a major instructional resource when and where it is used but that its function is very much like that of a textbook, an electronic textbook to be sure, but in terms of function it is very much like a textbook. What it does is to provide a regular resource where the youngsters and the teachers dip in and pull out some ideas which are then amplified through other application exercises, and that persists over the entire school year or half of it.

The notion of utility probably is best expressed in the notion of television providing concreteness to instruction on a regular basis. It seems to me that this is a complementation, in the sense of making whole. As I understand this use of the word, it is to add so that you make a whole. Historically words have been the dominant mode of instruction in our schools. Teachers have relied on the spoken, printed, and the written word. This has been the principal method of instruction.

Television over the last twenty or twenty-five years in the schools has added a dimension to instruction, and that dimension fundamentally has been to give more meaning to the word, to provide an opportunity for the youngster to arrive at abstraction by going through a chain of events, which Edgar Dale, one of our theoreticians in audiovisual education, called the cone of experience. In the cone you start at the bottom with direct experiencing and if you're fortunate you'll get to the very top, which is pure abstraction. In dealing with this continuum, schools can't always provide direct experience. They substitute vicarious experiences as a way of getting to abstractions. And it doesn't make any difference whether you're talking about a young person who is naive in a particular area or an older person at the sophomore level in college— if it's a new idea it generally has its own set of unknown concretenesses which have to be exposed, and in this sense television is probably adding that necessary complementation to the printed word.

Having said that, is television used, is it working in our schools? As of a year or so ago, the last definitive piece of evidence that we have, one-third of all our kindergarten through twelfth year students, about fifteen million, and their teachers were using about one hour of programs designed for the classroom per week over the entire school year. At the same time school systems were paying for a school television service for some twenty-two million youngsters. In other words, there was a gap between the number who were eligible to receive, for whom payment had been made—because this is a cost service, and schools don't get anything free either—at any rate, there was more paid for than they were using. Now this really is a remarkable figure because broadcast television—I'm only talking about the broadcast signal in usable form—is only available to about 70 percent of all schools, which is to say that about half of the schools are using it where it is available. Television is used in about half the classrooms where it is available.

School television programs are used repeatedly. If you take a given series the use of that series generally persists, like the life of a textbook, really, for about ten years. This extended use rests on the bedrock of merit. A teacher can be made aware of a school television series. A teacher can try it out, but a teacher cannot be compelled to continue the use. The reason that teachers persist in the use of a television series is really their perception that it is doing something desirable in their class. The reasons given by teachers for the continued use of material are that it is appealing to students—teachers like it too—but that it contributes to the work of the class and that it's so darned convenient. Administrators add, it is also economical.

This is broadcast television for the schools. We all like to dream, and I do too, about what's going to happen in the future, but generally speaking, the estimates of when that future will arrive are grossly exaggerated. None of us may be alive by the time that the use of prerecordings or recording off-the-air will equal the amount of use that we now have for broadcast television. What we would hope is that we are reaching a ceiling of the number of teachers who will want to use broadcasts in their classrooms. We've long since reached it at the secondary schools, where you have special problems of scheduling, multiple sections, instructors who are modeled after the professorial image, and all the rest. But in the elementary grades, where the same kids are typically learning the same things no matter where you are in the country, where the teacher has the impossible assignment of being expert in everything, the teacher welcomes television and will accommodate a broadcast if it does what the teacher wants within reasonable limits of the schedule. This schedule, by the way, has some flexibility, since each program is generally broadcast at several different times.

This is to say that at the present time television, I think, compared to other technologies like the film or audio recording, has made a remarkable penetration into American education, and the challenge really is how we can build from that outward.

THE PARENT, THE SCHOOL, AND THE TUBE

ANN P. KAHN

I think everyone is aware that the PTA has been involved for almost two years in an effort to remove excessive violence from television's entertainment programs. I am not going to discuss that campaign at this time. Anyone who is interested may send for our material. What I would like to share with you today are some of the "offshoots" of that effort that seem to have meaning for this seminar.

First of all, the antiviolence campaign has involved parents and teachers in a discussion of the impact of television on our lives. Millions of parents have begun, for the first time, to monitor television, watching what their children are watching and how their children are responding to what they watch.

We talked earlier today about who should accept the responsibility for what has happened to television. Everyone had a different idea. Let me tell you that, as a result of our campaign, many parents feel very strongly that they must accept the primary responsibility for what has happened to television. I think they do so in a sense that goes beyond their roles as parents; they are accepting this responsibility as citizens who want to have an impact on the world around them. To that degree their role then goes beyond such responses as "If you don't like it turn it off" or "Shut that television off and read a book instead, whether you like it or not" and indicates that parents agree that they have a responsibility to improve the quality of television and also to take a look at some of the broader questions relating to television.

First, parents and teachers became increasingly aware of the *amount* of time which young people, from very early preschool years all the way through high school years, are spending in front of the television set. Increasingly, we began hearing from parents who said that even if the quality were perfect, if everything that came over that set were fine and the kind of thing they'd like their children to be exposed to, there is still something very wrong when a five-year-old is watching an average of twenty-five hours and according to some surveys, as much as seventy hours of television a week. There is enormous competition for the time of a youngster and that kind of devotion to the television set, regardless of the quality of what comes over the tube, poses a serious threat to the youngsters' ability to learn and to grow and to do some of the things that childhood should involve.

The status of the family unit is threatened as well. I think that parents began to see that television was siphoning off a great deal of time that they felt youngsters should spend doing other things, including reading. There was great concern, for example, as to whether children in the early years were getting sufficient physical activity for proper physical growth when they sat plopped in front of the television set for many hours.

Everyone has talked about the degree to which extensive television watching is affecting imagination and creativity and the kinds of passivity that seem to be showing up in children's behavior. This too has been an enormous concern of both parents and teachers.

A second topic that rose to the surface concerned the impact of television on family life. Again, without regard to the quality of the programming, the worry was that children in this generation have, in effect, been raised by three parents, one of whom is electronic. Sometimes within the family structure there is an enormous conflict between the expectations of the natural parents regarding acceptable behavior and what a youngster learns from television as being "normal" and acceptable.

I think it's important that you not emphasize as much as you have here today a separation between educational television and entertainment-oriented television, because as far as a youngster is concerned, and I'm afraid as far as many adults are concerned also, there is no dichotomy; all television teaches. Whether it is intended to teach or not, television does teach, and as a result of its teaching, even when it's unintentional, youngsters particularly are learning much more than we may realize. Until parents begin to look at what is happening to their own children, I don't think most of them are aware of this fact. As a result of this monitoring, parents have begun to take a look at what it is their children are learning and, for the first time probably, discussing with their children what they have seen.

In order to get an honest picture of what their children absorb, we've asked parents who participated in this monitoring process, not to choose the programs that they would like their children to see, but instead to simply sit beside them and to watch what they are watching and then to discuss with them what they have learned from the program. For many parents this has been an exceedingly shocking process. We assume that youngsters are seeing things on television as we interpret those things through adult eyes, and it is rather eye-opening to go back and to listen to children discuss what *they* see.

An enormous concern has developed about what is happening to communication within the family. There is no question about it, when the family as a whole, or children in particular, spend enormous amounts of time watching television, communication among family members suffers. So does the art of conversation.

Parents indicated that when programming was shared between children and parents it often provided takeoff points for the kinds of conversations which many parents find difficult to initiate. Some parents mentioned that a particular program dealing with the death of a young child provided a good opportunity for discussion when parents and children viewed it together. In that sense, many parents found that this kind of programming was essentially very helpful to their jobs of being good parents.

A fourth point that has come to the surface, and we've discussed it somewhat today, is the need for public schools to begin to teach the skill of technical viewing. As a school board member, I know that for years the language-arts curriculum has focused on the ability of children to read a paragraph, to understand the relationship of one sentence to another, and to be able to judge whether a conclusion is justified by the preceding paragraph. Yet we have never advocated that kind of training for a generation that is *watching* as much as it is reading. We are now very much aware that parents and teachers want schools to teach those skills.

The impact of such a curriculum on a youngster's ability to view programs critically is enormous. Youngsters are very vulnerable to suggestion, so it's important to be able to teach the skill of critical questioning, and to do so in a way which permits rational judgments to follow. That skill has not yet been applied to television viewing. It has enormous repercussions, not the least of which will be the ability to develop skills that make children better consumers.

We're very concerned about how television has affected reading, and we've talked a great deal about that today, but we are also concerned about how television has affected writing. There has been an enormous deterioration of writing skills, and if you look at writing samples over a ten-year period within a single school, you can't help but be disturbed. Many parents are worried about their youngsters' inability to diagram or punctuate a sentence. I think these skills are really the least important. Of greater concern is the inability of many youngsters to express their thoughts in a coherent paragraph or to be able to organize their thoughts in a clear way. That skill really seems to be one which schools have not taught well, one which parents have not demanded, and one which is posing a really serious threat to literacy.

I can't neglect one other issue. I am very much aware of a growing concern among teachers about the use of television in the classroom. In many of our better schools there is a concern that a decision by school boards and superintendents to embrace the techniques of television in the classroom should be made with great caution, for we may very well be seeking a panacea which really does not exist. There is also some fear that in classrooms where the teaching level is poor, excessive use of television can shield against the improvement of teaching techniques.

Being a school board member in an area that has 164 schools in it, I do a great deal of driving. I like to pay attention to the bumper stickers that are on cars in front of me, and I find that there is a great deal of wisdom, and not a little bit of wit, in many of them. One that particularly intrigued me said, "You shall pay for your sins. If you have already paid, please disregard this notice."

In thinking about this subject, I'm not at all sure that we aren't as parents or as teachers or just as concerned citizens, perhaps "paying for our sins."

I leave you with one fundamental question that is critical to our discussion: what are the limits of television's role both in the school and in the family? Parents are asking this question and they are also telling us that the answer is more than a commercial decision. As we have discussed today, we have shared responsibilities in these matters, so we must come to shared decisions.

Discussion

Since the seminar was drawing to a close, Dr. Boorstin asked for comments from those who had not yet spoken. Linda Chavez of the American Federation of Teachers discussed AFT activities regarding the use of television in the classroom and called attention to articles and features in *American Education*, which she edits. Nancy Larrick pointed up several areas she felt had not been adequately discussed; the enormous effect of television characters such as Kotter, Kojak, and the Fonz on the language and behavior of preschool and elementary age children; the particular point of view of young parents and young teachers who themselves are products of the television age; and the way television affects a child's ability to learn. With regard to the last point, if a child has "had 5,000 hours of visual education before coming to school, how readily can he or she adjust to the linear, sequential kind of learning that is part of reading? How well can this child shift gears, "even with the best of teachers and all of the aids," to the type of verbal decoding that leads to the book? These and related questions are raised by Wilbur Schramm in his report on television and the Scholastic Aptitude Test scores. Lee Sauser reemphasized the importance of the copyright question and felt that additional seminars involving both educators and broadcasters are needed.

Henry Loomis expanded his earlier comments on the subject of rights. Most of the earlier discussion had centered on rights for off-the-air recording, and he did not think that was the answer. He said it was less important to guarantee CBS the exclusive use of a Bill Moyers documentary than it was to make it worth their while to sell a tape of that documentary—just as they sell books. When producers feel it is advantageous for them to create mechanisms necessary for effective and widespread distribution of their programs, television will have an opportunity to play a more serious role in the educational process. He also called for more research on "what kind of learning is particularly suitable for television, what is suitable for radio, [and] what is suitable for the printed word." The results would help us "select the media most suitable for the purpose we have in mind."

William Singer and Daniel Boorstin briefly discussed the copyright law and the rights issue. Mr. Singer, who explained that he was "clearly on the side of those who want to expand fair use or define it in a way that permits some off-air use," said that it will be quite difficult to bring about the needed legislative changes, primarily because of political power of those with vested interests. Clarification of the law was imperative, however, because many educators are now using the law as a "crutch." In other words, they are saying "I would use television if only I had the right to do so, if only the law were changed." Mr. Singer would like to remove that crutch. In response, Dr. Boorstin elaborated on his earlier comment about changing the copyright law:

> I did not mean to suggest that the law should be changed to give everybody a free ride, but rather to find new ways, ingenious ways which we have been working at in this country and on Capitol Hill for a long time, to use the laws to encourage the production, the remunerative, the profitable and effective and imaginative production of works of science and the useful arts. . . . The law has many sides and certainly we do not think of it as a way of destroying the property rights and incentives of individuals, but as ways of developing those rights in a way that will serve all of us more effectively, including ways to encourage people to produce more profitable works—television pro-

grams and those which will serve the public interest.

James Squire reminded the group that current research indicates that during the past six or seven years there has been a substantial improvement in the reading ability of children up to about the third or fourth grade. Television programs such as "Sesame Street" are one reason. But why does the improvement level off at about age ten? Wilbur Schramm's study, mentioned earlier by Nancy Larrick, suggests that at about the third grade level television may become a kind of opiate and even a counterproductive influence in terms of learning and instruction. More research is needed about instructional educational television: what is its place in the developmental scheme of learning and at what grade levels is it the most effective?

Edward S. Stanley mentioned two other areas that provide great opportunities for using television in the educational process: continuing education for professionals, e.g., doctors, accountants, and judges, and "lifetime learning" programs directed at the growing audience of older Americans who enjoy learning but are not affiliated with universities or colleges. Commissioner Washburn stressed the mutual responsibilities of teachers, broadcasters, librarians, parents, activist groups, government, and even television sponsors to integrate television and the printed word into the educational process. He called for a study concerning the long-range financial support that will be needed to provide the teaching materials to be used in this expanded effort.

Dr. Boorstin concluded the seminar by referring to the "cheering announcement" made by the Office of Education of its proposal for linking television, books, and the printed word in the classroom. He also reminded the seminar participants

> that part of the mandate of the Library of Congress is not to do anything that can be done by private

enterprise. And one of our purposes in this country is to encourage people to invent enterprises which ought to be profitable and, we would hope, promote our common interests. That is how this country has grown, and that is how it will continue to grow. And it seems to me that this is the challenge of television to all of us, to find ways to promote activities which can be both rewarding to individuals and rewarding to the community.

Appendix 1

PARTICIPANTS

Mortimer Adler
educator
Director, Institute for
Philosophical Research

Lester Asheim
Professor, School of
Library Science
University of North Carolina

Erik Barnouw
author and critic

Daniel J. Boorstin
The Librarian of Congress

Ernest L. Boyer
U.S. Commissioner of
Education

Brian Brightley
Coordinator, Special Projects/
Educational Activities
Corporation for Public
Broadcasting

Kathryn F. Broman
President
Springfield TV, Inc.
Springfield, Massachusetts

Cyril Busbee
Superintendent of Education
South Carolina

Peggy Charren
President
Action for Children's TV

Linda Chavez
Director of Communications
American Federation of
Teachers

Edwin G. Cohen
Executive Director
Agency for Instructional TV

Marcus Cohn
Partner
Cohn and Marks,
Washington, D.C.

Roy Danish
Director
Television Information Office
of the National Association
of Broadcasters

Robert Geller
Director
Learning in Focus, Inc.

Grace Hechinger
author

Howard Hitchens
Executive Director
Association for Education
Communications and
Technology

Paul L. Houts
Director of Publications
and Editor
The National Elementary
Principal

Ann Kahn
National Secretary
National Parent Teacher
Association

Karen Klass
Communications Specialist
National Education
Association

Dan Lacy
Senior Vice President
McGraw-Hill, Inc.

Nancy Larrick
Adjunct Professor of
Education
Lehigh University

Sharon Lerner
Vice President
Children's Television
  Workshop

Tom Litzenburg
Special Assistant to the
  Chairman
National Endowment for
  the Humanities

Robert K. Logan
Department of Physics
University of Toronto

Henry Loomis
President
Corporation for Public
  Broadcasting

Michael J. McAndrew
Director, Educative Services
Capital Cities Television
  Productions

Margaret McNamara
Chairman of the Board
Reading is Fundamental, Inc.

Gene Mater
Vice President and Assistant
  to the President
CBS/Broadcast Group

William S. Rubens
Vice President of Research
  and Planning
National Broadcasting
  Company

Lee Sauser
Director of Educative Services
Public Broadcasting Service

Steven H. Scheuer
Editor and Publisher
TV Key

William S. Singer
President
Prime Time School Television

Robert Sklar
Chairman, Department of
  Cinema Studies
New York University

James R. Squire
Senior Vice President and
  Publisher
Ginn and Company

Ralph C. Staiger
Executive Director
International Reading
  Association

Edward Stanley
President
Teachers Guides to Television

Frank Stanton
Former President of CBS

Donald Thurston
Chairman of the Board
National Association of
  Broadcasters

Carll Tucker
Chairman of the Board
Saturday Review

Pam Warford
Manager of Community
  Relations
American Broadcasting
  Company

Abbott M. Washburn
Commissioner
Federal Communications
  Commission

Appendix 2
Education in the Electronic Society
by John Platt

(Editor's note: **John Platt, lecturer in the Departments of Anthropology and Environmental Studies at the University of California at Santa Barbara, was unable to attend the seminar but submitted a provocative paper for distribution as background reading. "Education in the Electronic Society" is mentioned several times in the proceedings and Dr. Platt kindly has granted permission for its inclusion in this volume. It is based on his contribution to a series of seminars held in early 1978 by the National Institute of Education on new technological opportunities in education. "Education in the Electronic Society" will be published in abridged form in a late 1978 issue of the** Bulletin of Atomic Scientists.)

What new directions of education will we need for a world linked together by electronic media from the cradle to the grave?

All around us the electronic society is coming into being. Television and computers have changed our daily life and work, our ways of thinking, and our political and global sensibilities. Yet the educational system, whose primary concern should be with preparing for the future, seems to be the last to recognize these changes. It is time to look with fresh eyes at these new patterns of communication and interaction to see where they are leading us and what education could do and should do in the world they are making.

The Electronic Surround

It is important to realize how far we have gone in the new direction. We are living already in what McLuhan has called the Electronic Surround. Half of the jobs in the American economy are now "tertiary" or information-handling jobs, and more and more of them have become computerized or electronic. Banks and businesses are linked together by credit cards and data processing. Government records, science, and the military are all dependent on big computers. Everywhere there are pocket calculators, transistor radios, citizens' band radios, and stereo sets with records and tapes. We have electronic monitors in stores and entryways, and videotapes for learning tennis. Telephone and television are linked by global satellites, while the home begins to have two-way cable, electronic games, and video recordings on cassettes and disks.

In our personal lives, television expands to fill the available time. Americans watch it for an average of four hours per day per person, or for more than half of their leisure time. Canadians and Japanese spend even more time on it, and of course particular groups in our society, such as housewives, children, the old, the sick, the unemployed, and people in the ghetto, watch for much longer hours. During blackouts, the looting in the ghetto is surely partly due to the fact that the television has gone off and people suddenly have nothing else to do.

Today it is estimated that most children have watched three thousand to four thousand hours of TV before they start the first grade, and thereafter they put in more hours watching it than they do in school. This pattern is now spreading rapidly around the world, because television is the cheapest way of spending time that the human race has ever devised. It costs only a few cents per person per day, including power and programming. It is often cheaper than the chair we watch it in, a hundred times cheaper than a car and a thousand times cheaper than a teacher. Even the poorest countries are beginning to take it up, because it is the fastest way of upgrading skills, literacy, health, and productivity for millions of people who have no teachers or doctors and cannot read. It has been estimated that by 1980 in many parts of Asia, Africa, and Latin American, the average eighteen-year-old will already have seen eighteen thousand hours of television, and that the 1980 Olympic Games in Moscow will be watched by 2 billion people, nearly half the human race.

This level of immersion in television has many troubling aspects, of course. Thoughtful people deplore and fear its violent programs and commercialization or its government propaganda and censorship, and its hypotic effects, especially on children. But the electronic media are surely here to stay, and what we must do is to find out how to understand and control them and how to use their real potentialities for human development.

Certainly television enlarges our world and links us more closely together. All human beings become parts of a simultaneous emotional response network. It is said that children in the first grade now know the meaning of many more words than children knew in 1900. How could they help it, after being exposed to all that diversity and life? Even adventure shows and old Westerns expand their horizons. And from age two to eighty-two, with TV debates and news, we have all learned about space, oceans, the environment, the limits to growth, energy, nuclear dangers, the antiwar movement, Watergate and the constitutional process, the Third World and hunger, women's liberation, and so on and on for dozens of major social and political issues that were not taught in disciplinary courses or in schools and colleges at all, until the students themselves insisted that they be brought into the classrooms.

The electronic media have had cultural impacts that the earlier critics did not anticipate. Have mathematics skills decreased? Perhaps, but there are more computer users and computer programmers than we could have imagined. Has television overemphasized professional sports? Perhaps, but jogging and swimming and tennis and soccer are booming. Have reading skills decreased? Is culture lost? Perhaps, but more people have read *The Forsyte Saga* and *I, Claudius* than ever before, more have seen a Shakespeare play in a single evening than in all the previous centuries, and symphony orchestras and ballet companies are multiplying everywhere. We do well to be concerned, and there are interests of the mind that we may have to make special efforts to keep alive, but the balance of cultural excellence, diversity, and participation is not necessarily on the side of the preelectronic age.

What Future for the Schools?

Yet we are just at the beginning of this electronic era. Is it not likely that the eventual effects on personal and global consciousness will be even greater, especially when two-way cable and electronic games and cassettes and disks begin to give us more diversity and personalization? We are suddenly brought straight up against the question, What function will schools continue to have in such a world where reading, writing, and arithmetic and the older disciplines have become so oddly irrelevant and the interesting stimulation and education all seems to be outside? Will the schools become mere holding tanks for children? Quaint relics of an earlier system? Or an elite service for the well-born, as they were two centuries ago?

Surely our educational system can play a far more central role than this, if we want it to. But for it to reassume leadership in an electronic world, we must stop thinking of it as nothing but classrooms, teachers, and books. The mission of the educational system should be to teach all of our children and adults as effectively as possible and by every available method what they need to know to reach their full potential as human beings and citizens.

To do this today would require us to bring together much more successfully the schools and the media. Formal learning and teaching will have to start taking the Electronic Surround into account in a central way. It will have to realize that it is dealing with a new kind of student, needing new content, new methods, new training, and a continual reeducation outside the schoolroom for all of life. The schools and the universities will need to mobilize their resources to help adults as well as children understand this rapidly changing society, with its new technologies and new global problems, and prepare to anticipate and deal with the still newer problems of 1990 to 2040 when these children will have become the decision-making adults.

Managing any such program successfully will take far more research than we have devoted to it. It will take debate and planning and research on individual and group behavior and learning in this electronic environment. We will need our best forecasting and our best insights, and thousands of experiments and pilot projects to try out and evaluate alternative approaches.

But with such a change of attitude and effort, six or seven areas leap to mind where formal education could begin to make itself much more effective and could take leadership in the transformation of the larger society.

The Aware Schoolroom

The first thing that existing schools can do is to be aware of the ongoing electronic world around them, to amplify and explain the issues it brings before us, and to try to correct and compensate for some of its dangers and shortcomings.

Good schools and good teachers do this already on a large scale, as they did in the days of radio and newspapers. A television program such as "Roots," which ran for six nights in a row and reached eighty million U.S. viewers, has provided stimulus and material for analysis in geography, history, and social science, as well as poetry and literature. An exciting curriculum in the social sciences could be built around major TV programs, with added library materials and community discussions. With a little more effort, the same could be done for programs involving engineering and the biological sciences, and for music and art and literature, although the coverage here might be rather spotty and unsystematic.

The schools might make better use of such nationwide programs when they are first presented, if they could mobilize national experts, on a few days' notice, to provide background and enrichment materials. This could be a fairly inexpensive way of increasing the excitement of the schoolroom and its sense of relevance to the world, for schools all over the country. In many cases, the cost might even be supported by the sponsors of the program, as part of their institutional advertising, although adequate controls to ensure the impartiality and academic quality of such background materials would be essential.

But it is important not to deal with first-graders as though they had not seen "Sesame Street," or with high-schoolers as though they had not seen space flights.

The Electronic Schoolroom

The use of the new electronic devices in the schoolroom itself has been widely discussed and does not need to be elaborated here, where we are concerned with the broader educational mission. Many groups are now developing the use of classroom television, including central broadcasting of programs, videotapes for learning new skills, cassettes and disks for whole libraries of lectures and background films and other materials, two-way television for interactive discussions and questions, responsive games and computerized learning systems like the PLATO system at the University of Illinois, language tapes, and personalized learning programs with instant reinforcement for individual students progressing at their own rate. No doubt these will all be fitted into the classroom of the future in one way or another. The role of the human teacher may come to be that of more personalized help and clarification, of setting things into a larger context and a larger philosophy. The teaching task itself may also be simplified and helped by the use of similar electronic preparation and materials and by video examples of effective classroom methods, if such materials can be prepared on a national scale.

A Curriculum for the New World

What has not yet been done is the development of a whole curriculum appropriate to this new world, to teach young citizens how to participate in its life and work and play. What old subjects can or should be dropped? What new subjects or approaches should be especially emphasized?

These are questions for intense debate, and the debates will probably be politicized, with very different attitudes and answers between conservatives and liberals or between groups with different opinions on ecology or economics or technology or social and political change. And the choices that are made will probably change continually as knowledge and civic needs change in every decade. We can see this simply by comparing our educational emphases in 1978 with those in 1968. At that time our eyes were fixed on space, civil rights, the Vietnam war, and student protests, and there was still little interest in those new subjects of ecology and pollution, energy, the limits to growth, the problems of cities, school reform, busing, sexual freedom, birth control, abortions, women's liberation and affirmative action, and religious reform. In the last ten years, all these have become subjects of intense debate, concern, and violence. The controversies over them have changed the relation of schools to students and to the community and the law, and they have changed the internal curriculum, from universities down to grade schools, not only in the United States but around the world. After such a decade, we should at least try to think about what 1988 will call for that will be different still.

What shall we do about the more traditional subjects?

In a world of electric typewriters, how much handwriting does a child need to learn? How much does the average adult still use?

With the best television teaching, how much of our emphasis on reading comprehension will become clumsy and obsolete, blocking skills and knowledge that could be learned easily by visual demonstration? If new audiovisual methods are more effective for industrial or managerial training, would they not also be more effective for students in school?

With seven-place pocket calculators costing less than five dollars, and with computers at every checkout counter, how much rote multiplication, long division, complex fractions, or logarithms are desirable, of the kind that have frightened most children and adults away from mathematics? How much complex mathematics does the average adult need or use today?

At a higher level, if most jobs will involve the handling of information, what vocational skills should we teach? Should it be shorthand, or word processing? Double-entry bookkeeping, or computer programming? Shop skills, or video reporting? In research and professional training, should students learn particular skills, or learn to learn, so that later they can master updated video instructions as the disciplines change over the years? Should we use language texts, or tapes? Geometry and engineering drawings, or electronic geometry games and the construction of Fuller domes? History and art and music lectures, or a great systematic series of videocassettes and videodisks?

If we can drop and compress some of the older materials and make room for them, there are several important new disciplines of the last few years that could and should be introduced at high school level. These include the new biological integration, the new psychology, and the computer simulations of global systems and changes, all of which can help students understand themselves and this new world much better. New fields that can be made vivid and exciting at the junior high school level include the sociobiology of the social animals, the new geology, with its great continental plates sliding under each other, and the new astronomy, with space explorations and strange radio stars.

Probably we should also begin to make room for some of the integrative ideas that C. H. Waddington has listed in his last book, *Tools of Thought,* such as feedback, information theory, and how to handle information overload; chain reactions with growth and decay, as applied to nuclear reactions, biological growth, business cycles, or human history; and ecological interactions and systems analysis. These are the major systems tools for an interactive computer age, and they can be taught conceptually and practically with only the simplest mathematics. Teachers themselves also need to know these subjects, both for personal understanding and management and professional application.

New Modes of Awareness

The schools will have to incorporate new ways of looking at things and doing things. McLuhan more than anyone else has emphasized the change in our mental processes that must come as we shift from print to television. It is happening already. Our imaging and learning and our linking to each other cannot help but be transformed as our mental inputs change. Verbal argument and books, with their linear and sequential information, speak to the "left brain," while motion pictures and television, with their high-information holistic moving-field patterns in space, develop the powers of the "right brain." Print is private, interiorized, and analytical; video is public, externalized, and impressionistic. The new media take us back toward the primary human modes of communicating emotion and information through dance, ritual, and drama. Learning comes to be again by imitation and apprenticeship, whether it is practicing yoga or Japanese brush painting or cooking with Julia.

The change to a generation of students for whom this has been the dominant mode of relationship and learning since infancy cannot help but force changes in schools, classrooms, teachers, materials, and methods, although it is not clear what these changes will eventually be. Probably some educators will try to make the school experience as much like the TV as possible, to capitalize on the transfer of learning modes. Others may try to make it as different as possible, to try to preserve the bookish and analytical skills. Or possibly some new and better ways will be invented that can combine these values. The emotional involvement of the television image might be used with something like split-screen methods to sharpen up alternatives and to make complex relations clearer or conclusions more convincing. This is evidently a most important area for research contracts and pilot studies with careful evaluations.

The future of books and of libraries of books in this new electronic world is a subject fraught with emotion. We have loved books for two thousand years, and rightly so, for their enormous transformation of human understanding and the human condition. They have brought us culture and cultural change and diversity. We have treasured their privacy, for private entertainment or private dissent from the official dogma or private sharing with a special friend. We have come to equate intellect with letters.

Yet we bookish people have almost forgotten that the humanities, including poetry, history, and drama, and the philosophy and religion of Socrates and Jesus, with their dialogues and parables, were originally oral and representational and did not need written symbols for their thought. It is mathematics and the sciences that would have been greatly retarded without symbolic lines and letters.

Undoubtedly books will never die out, neither the sciences nor the humanities, and libraries will continue growing in size and complexity. But probably in an electronic era, books and written records will be relegated increasingly to reference functions carried on by specialists. The oral and visual communication of human ideas, like the active records and work of the world, in enormously increased volume, will not be left in libraries but will be carried everywhere on tape and disk for the computer and the screen, with instant access from every home or office.

This effective "end of the era of books" may still be a generation away for us in the industrial societies. But for a billion and a half people in the Third World, the transition may come in the next few years, straight from a village oral tradition to a television oral-and-demonstration tradition, without ever passing through the era of books and literacy. In fact, the necessity of writing software programs to teach *everything* by television to nonliterates, either in the developing countries or in our own, cannot help but speed up the transition away from books for the rest of us. Early educational programs will come to teach skills, complex relations, and social values far more important to society than the alphabet.

As it makes these changes in our perceptions and modes of interaction, television will bring us for the first time a wholly nonpunitive education. It is a change that the schools will surely have to incorporate. The TV screen has no truant officer, no school compulsion, no rap on the knuckles or being kept after school or bad grades or parental scolding, to force its viewers to stay in their seats and to pay attention. It has only its own interest and build-up, second by second, to hold them—that is, in Skinnerian terms, its instant positive reinforcement for continuing to watch.

As Skinner has shown, no punitive method can compete with such an attractive system, for creating interest, modifying behavior and attitudes, and learning. The schools will not be able to compete with the power of television until they begin to create their own continuously attractive programs, live or video, building in the same instant-by-instant fascination so that they do not need to depend at all on the remnants of compulsion that are still in use today. This may be one of the most difficult emotional points for schools of education and for traditional teachers to understand and believe in and learn to practice, but it is a necessary key to education in the Electronic Surround.

Finally, the sense of human relationship and global relationship is something that the electronic world has given us on a scale we never had before. This may seem a strange observation when we think how disembodied the voices are that we hear on the radio, or how detached and artificial the images and people on the screen often seem. But they represent a world larger and older than the family or the village night, stretching to Washington or to the moon, or years into the vanished past. And with habit, they become more real and more important than the family, as the current war or oil spill comes nightly to our dinner table. We all follow Claudius together or stand with hope beside Sadat in Jerusalem. We become both more global and more individualized, as we link up with other groups with the same backgrounds and interests, whether they are other nuclear protesters or tennis buffs or ethnic groups or liberated women or evangelical believers.

This outreach makes most textbooks and teaching materials today seem limited and stereotyped. And all of these enticements to identify with a wider but more personally interesting world will increase with the new developments such as more diverse programming, two-way cable television, special-interest electronic games, and individualized videocassettes or disks with libraries of programs. A precursor of this kind is the "Thinker's Tournament" program of mathematical games between schools in Ann Arbor and other Michigan cities, which uses cable television and conference telephone. Teachers might find such links extremely valuable professionally, especially in dealing with new program material used in many schools at once.

Using the Electronic Surround

Does it not seem likely that the more progressive schools will then move on to the central and systematic use of the electronic media as a high-quality core and universal resource for all their work? With leadership, they will begin to work in advance with broadcasters and public and educational networks to build courses around such serials as "Sesame Street" and "The Electric Company" for younger children, and "Civilization," "The Ascent of Man," and "Roots" for older ones. They will solve the copyright and cost problems so that they can build libraries of videocassettes and disks, available like books for study or review by anyone at any time. Athletic teams, musicians, actors, and debaters will correct their errors and improve performance rapidly by watching their own videotapes with instant replay and slow motion. Teachers could profitably do the same to improve their own classroom performance. A major part of the curricula in the teachers' colleges may be devoted to learning how to use all these media effectively. These possibilities have been talked about, and both exaggerated and belittled, for many years, but most educators have not realized how rapidly and universally they will come, as electronic hardware becomes cheaper than seats and books.

Creating New Electronic Education
for Schools and the Public

As all this begins to happen, these new media will begin to be taken over and developed for education in a comprehensive way, as an intellectual and experiential feast, rather than as crumbs from the table of the broadcasters. The planning and initial steps toward this development cannot begin too soon, for the time and the need, and perhaps the money, are already here.

A reminder about economics may be helpful. Because programs can be reused indefinitely, the software costs of electronic education will go down even more dramatically in the long run than their hardware costs. This is true even with elaborate planning and highly selected video teachers and the best media technology. When we consider the 30 million children who have learned the alphabet and numbers from "Sesame Street" in the last ten years, the $8 million cost of creating the initial series works out to about three cents per child per hour—the cheapest method of early education ever devised.

Education is now a $100 billion operation. It is the largest industry in the U.S., and now the largest industry in the world, surpassing even military expenditures after 1974, according to United Nations statistics. If we had the leadership to use even part of 1 percent of this budget to get a consortium of schools and colleges and government agencies and foundations to begin producing the electronic educational feast, it would generate a national and world transformation.

In short, the educational system could begin to be its own producer and programmer. It will have to create entertainment, of course, effectively and self-sustainingly, but its basic goals will be learning, remembering and using, and for these purposes it will have to find its own new mixes of media, its own content and standards and pace, and its own full curricula for all ages of students.

The best of public television has begun to do this now. Increasingly, these enjoyable learning programs will burst out of the nine-to-four school day and over school walls into homes and conference centers and by satellite around the world.

As it reaches a larger public, this move away from the era of books will change social institutions as well as modes of awareness. We do not often consider what rather special human patterns the invention of writing has created over several thousand years. Putting marks on paper to represent speech led to the alphabet and then to books and printing and libraries. It was unnatural and hard to learn, so it led to years of formal schooling, first for an elite class of scribes and then for all children in a democracy. It required specially trained teachers to read from books or to dictate for copying, often with canings and tears. The result now is the whole apparatus of school buildings and classes and exams, and busing and lunch programs, and truant officers and schools of education—and a total change in the meaning of childhood and the natural ways of learning from adults by doing.

But if we begin to introduce electronic images effectively in place of books, much of this clumsy machinery of learning can be gotten rid of as being inefficient, coercive, and dull. It does not show us how to do anything well—to build cars or run a bank or speak a language, or even read books. Its helps to create bored and hostile teenagers who know nothing of the work of the world and who actively hate mathematics and physics and English and poetry and music. How can we go on supporting these economic and social costs, if better ways are available?

Massive electronic education will have its problems, too, as we are constantly reminded, but at least they are different problems as the walls of the classroom disappear. And this non-coercive medium that can teach anyone who watches, old or young, by fascination alone, also has enormous strengths and creative potential. It is a power for individual and social change that we can capture and master if we act now. Homework can become home play. Self-teaching and skills, and a common base of knowledge and concern and a common ground of dialogue might be brought back. The electronic living notebooks might facilitate all our activities and might become the daily reality of continuing education.

The Never-Ending Education of the Whole Society

Our new technological powers and our new intensities of communication and interaction around the world have moved us toward a self-transforming society. We are becoming, both nationally and globally, a cybernetic society that chooses its own goals deliberately. Nowadays we are rejecting in advance this or that technology or structure and demanding research and development of other methods that will take us closer to where we want to go. This is the meaning of the protest movements and the World Bank; of the blocking of the supersonic transport and the new research on solar energy; of the demand for public accountability and the human rights movement.

At the heart of such a society must be a continual ongoing education in new ways and a continual informed debate over new goals. Only the electronic media can reach throughout such a society fast enough and completely enough—changing all ages together—to make this kind of self-transformation possible. But the media presentations in this mutual education must be based on the best library materials and the best experts and teachers and the best teaching methods, if we are to avoid sensationalism or commercialism.

What this means is that such a continual reeducation of ourselves as a public must be integrated into, and must be a major part of, the whole educational enterprise. Already the universities have a majority of their enrollments outside the traditional eighteen to twenty-two year age bracket, and in Britain, the Open University with television classes is a major scholastic enterprise. This may be the beginning of the turnaround, as we come to see the primary educational mission as the never-ending education of the whole society, and as schools become radio and television centers and conference and adult education centers for everybody. The special education of the young is only a fraction of this mission, and the continuation of traditional teaching with books and schoolrooms will be a smaller fraction still.

Such a transformation toward truly holistic education using all of our networks will take years of leadership and dedicated effort. But is not this the natural direction of the whole electronic world with its immediacy, its universality, its emotional involvement, and its differentiated special interests? It may be that the greatest educators of the future will come to be the greatest producers, directors, and teachers reaching out to everyone through the media and educating the world—and the young along with everybody else.

Appendix 3

Guide to Further Information
Compiled by Jean Johnson,
*Resource Director, Action
for Children's Television*

I. TELEVISION AND EDUCATION

PUBLICATIONS

American Educator. American Federation of Teachers, AFL-CIO, 11 Dupont Circle NW, Washington, D.C., (202) 797-4400. A regular television supplement that includes guides to upcoming programming and ideas on ways to use television with children. Quarterly; $2.50 per year.

Artel, Linda. "Films about Television." **Sightlines,** Winter 1977/78, pp. 17-22. A selected list of films dealing with television history, production, economics, and its social impact.

Boyle, Deirdre. "The Library, Television, and the Unconscious Mind." **Wilson Library Bulletin,** May 1978, pp. 696-702. An interesting discussion of librarians' attitudes toward television and other visual media.

Byars, Betsy. **The TV Kid.** New York: Viking Press, 1976. 123 pages. $6.50. A short novel for children (eight through thirteen) that can encourage discussion of television and its not-so-subtle messages. Illustrated by Richard Cuffari.

Center for Understanding Media. **Doing the Media: A Portfolio of Activities and Resources.** New York, 1972. 219 pp. $5. A special section includes a discussion of ways in which using video equipment can help students become more critical viewers.

"Children and Television—Concerns of the School Media Specialist." **School Media Quarterly** 5, no. 3 (Spring 1977). A special issue devoted to the topic.

Dalziel, Bonnie. "Exit Dick and Jane?" **American Education,** July 1976, pp. 9-13. A discussion of how commercial television programs such as "Eleanor and Franklin" can be used to improve reading skills.

"The Ecology of Education: Television." **The National Elementary Principal** 56, no. 3 (January/February 1977). 104 pp. $4.00 A special issue on television and learning. Television's effect on children is examined in more than a dozen essays by noted authorities. Available from the National Association of Elementary School Principals, 1801 N. Moore St., Arlington, Virginia 22209.

Heintz, Ann Christine. **Persuasion.** Chicago: Loyola University Press, 1974. 224 pp. $3.20. A secondary level text on the strategies of advertising. The volume contains several ideas that can be adapted for use with young students.

Heintz, Ann Christine. "Using What Kids Watch on TV." **Media and Methods,** March 1976, pp. 42ff. An article that suggests ways to use popular television series in the classroom.

Heintz, Ann Christine, Laurence M. Reuter, and Elizabeth Conley. **Mass Media: A Worktext in the Processes of Modern Communication.** Chicago; Loyola University Press, 1975. 240 pp. $3.50. A secondary level text on mass communications that can be adapted for younger students.

Kuhns, William. **Exploring Television.** Chicago; Loyola University Press, 1975. 240 pp. $3.50. A secondary level text that stresses the development of critical viewing skills.

Laybourne, Kit. "A Television Atlas." **Sightlines,** Winter 1977/78, pp. 8-10. A suggested course of study that examines television as a political, social, and economic force.

Littell, Joseph F., ed. **Coping with Television.** Evanston, Ill.: McDougal Littell, 1973. 213 pp. $3.87. A secondary level text with readings on commercial programming and news coverage, public television, and audience response. Some sections of the text may be adapted for the intermediate grades.

Markham, Lois B. "How to Make Commercial TV Work for You." **Scholastic Teacher,** November-December 1974, pp. 8-13. An article containing suggestions for using popular television series such as "Little House on the Prairie."

Media Mix. Claretian Publications, 221 W. Madison St., Chicago, Ill. 60606. A monthly newsletter that regularly features information for educators about incorporating TV into the school curriculum.

O'Brien, Clare Lynch. "Using Commercial TV in the Classroom." **Teacher,** September 1976, pp. 45-52. An article containing ideas for discussing news programming, situation comedies, fantasy series, and sports programs with elementary school students.

O'Bryant, Shirley L., and Charles R. Corder-Bolz. "Children and Television," **Children Today,** May/June 1978, pp. 21-24. A discussion of practical ways parents and teachers can mediate children's television viewing.

Potter, Rosemary Lee. **New Season: The Positive Use of Commercial Television with Children.** Columbus, Ohio: Charles E. Merrill, 1976. 126 pp. $3.95. A book featuring lesson plans based on commercial television for use with elementary school children.

Prime Time School Television. **Television, Police, and the Law.** Niles, Ill.: Argus Communications, 1977. $4.50. A curriculum unit using popular television police shows to encourage discussion about law enforcement and civil rights.

Schrank, Jeffrey. **TV Action Book.** Evanston, Ill.: McDouglas Littell, 1976. 127 pp. $2.35. A secondary level text that emphasizes consumer rights in broadcasting. It is part of **Television and Values,** a multimedia kit that includes a filmstrip, a cassette, project cards, and a teaching guide. The kit is available from the Learning Seed Company, 145 Brentwood Dr., Palatine, Ill. 60067. $38.60.

Seward, Stephen. "Books as Television Best Sellers, or Give That TV Addict a Book!" **Wilson Library Bulletin,** November 1977, pp. 232-36. A discussion of the use of novels and non-fiction best-sellers for television plots and the implications of this particular trend.

Skinner, Stanley. **The Advertisement Book.** Evanston, Ill.: McDougal Littell, 1976. 153 pp. $2.88. A secondary level text on advertising messages. The text contains some lesson ideas that may also be appropriate for junior high students; many sections can be adapted for younger students.

Sohn, David. **The Problem and the Promise: A Television/ Video Workshop.** Santa Monica, Calif.: Pyramid Films, 1978. 31 pp. A film-based curriculum unit which examines television advertising, programming, and news coverage. It includes a bibliography.

Teacher. Macmillan Professional Magazines, 1 Fawcett Place, Greenwich, Conn. 06830. The magazine's regular column, "TV Talk," includes ideas for elementary school teachers. Monthly; $12 per year.

Teachers Guides to Television. 699 Madison Avenue, New York, N.Y. 10021. A teacher's guide to upcoming television specials and other programs of interest, published twice during the school year. $4 per year.

Television Awareness Training. New York, N.Y.: Media Action Research Center, 1977. 304 pp. $8.00. A workbook and text developed by the United Methodist Church, American Lutheran Church, Church of the Brethren, and Media Action Research Center. It includes collected TV essays from a wide variety of sources and provides an informative stimulus for high school/adult discussions about the medium.

FILMS

Seeing Through Commercials: A Children's Guide to TV Advertising. A fifteen-minute, 16mm color film with sound that demystifies television commercials by illustrating and discussing advertising techniques. It is appropriate for grades three through eight. The film is available from Vision Films, P. O. Box 48896, Los Angeles, Calif. 90048. Rental, $25; purchase, $225.

Six Billion $$$ Sell: A Child's Guide to TV Commercials. A fifteen-minute, 16mm color film with sound that uses clips from television commercials, animation, and an original pop theme song to teach children about the techniques used by advertisers. It is appropriate for grades three through eight. The film is available from Consumer Reports Films, Box XA-35, 256 Washington Street, Mount Vernon, N. Y. 10550. Rental, $25; purchase, $220.

Supergoop. A thirteen-minte, 16mm color film with sound that tells an animated story about a marketing and advertising campaign for a new sugared cereal, "Supergoop." The film is appropriate for grades three through six. It is available from Churchill Films, 662 N. Robertson Blvd., Los Angeles, Calif. 90069. Rental, $18, purchase, $190.

ORGANIZATIONS

Action for Children's Television, 46 Austin Street, Newtonville, Mass. 02160, (617) 527-7870. ACT is a national consumer organization working for quality television without commercialism for children. It sponsors research on children's television, publishes materials relating to children and television, and maintains a specialized research library. Membership in ACT costs $15 annually and includes a subscription to **re:act,** ACT's quarterly news magazine.

Children's Television Workshop, 1 Lincoln Plaza, New York, N.Y. 10023, (212) 595-3456. CTW's Community Education Services Division develops supplemental teaching tools for use with "Sesame Street," "Electric Company," and other CTW productions. Currently available are **SESAME STREET Script Highlights** ($5) and **SESAME STREET Activities Manual** ($1).

National Parent-Teacher Association, 700 Rush Street, Chicago, Ill. 60611. (312) 787-0977. The National PTA's TV Project is coordinating efforts to reduce violence in television programming. Other TV-related activities are also under way.

Prime Time School Television, Suite 810, 120 S. LaSalle St., Chicago, Ill. 60603, (312) 368-1088. PTST publishes monthly bulletins supplying information for teachers about prime time programs and their uses as educational resources. **The Creative Handbook,** published quarterly, features ideas for parents and teachers. PTST plans future curriculum units on TV economics, parenting, and values.

Teachers Guides to Television, 699 Madison Avenue, New York, N.Y. 10021, (212) 249-2249. This organization publishes TV-related educational materials. With NBC-TV, it coordinates "Parent Participation TV Workshops" across the country.

Television Information Office, 745 Fifth Avenue, New York, N.Y. 10022. (212) 759-6800. The TIO is an information service sponsored by the television networks, local stations, and the National Association of Broadcasters. It maintains a library and publishes a variety of materials relating to television. Local public television stations can often provide information about supplementary materials for PBS series such as "Vegetable Soup," "Infinity Factory," "Carrascolendas," and "As•We•See•It." Cooperating stations and names of coordinators can be found in the **Educative Services Directory,** available from Public Broadcasting Service, 475 L'Enfant Plaza West, SW, Washington, D.C. 20024, (202) 488-5000.

II. TELEVISION'S EFFECT ON CHILDREN

PUBLICATIONS

Kaye, Evelyn. **Family Guide to Children's Television: What to Watch, What to Miss, What to Change and How to Do It.** New York: Pantheon Books, 1974. 194 pp. $2.95. Also available from Action for Children's Television. Discusses major issues in children's television and proposes strategies for change; a "Children's Workbook" section is included.

Larrick, Nancy. "Children of Television." **A Parent's Guide to Children's Reading.** 4th ed. New York: Bantam Books, 1975. A discussion of television's effect on children, with suggestions for parents on how to handle problems related to television watching.

Leifer, Aimee Dorr, Neal J. Gordon, and Sherryl Browne Graves. "Children's Television: More than Mere Entertainment." **Harvard Educational Review** 44 (1974): 213-45. A review of the literature concerned with "social messages" on television.

Liebert, Robert M., John M. Neale, and Emily S. Davidson. **The Early Window: Effects of TV on Children and Youth.** New York: Pergamon Press, 1973. 133 pp. $6.50. An informative survey of research on television and children and an analysis of the research relating to television violence and children.

Mukerji, Rose. "TV's Impact on Children: A Checkerboard Scene." **Phi Delta Kappan,** January 1976, pp. 316-21. A review of the research on television's effect on the early childhood years.

Schramm, Wilbur. **Television and the Test Scores.** Princeton, N.J.: College Board Publications, 1977. 18 pp. $2.00. A report on television's effect on reading, prepared for the Advisory Panel on the Scholastic Aptitude Test Score Decline.

FILMS

But First This Message. A fifteen-minute, 16mm color film with sound that includes film clips from children's television programs and commercials and statements from children, physicians, a toy manufacturer, a professor of communications, and a professor of child development. The film is appropriate for high school and adult audiences. It is available from Action for Children's Television, 46 Austin St., Newtonville, Mass. 02160. Rental, $25; purchase, $185.

It's as Easy as Selling Candy to a Baby. An eleven-minute 16mm color film with sound that includes film clips of television food ads directed to children and a discussion of the influence of advertising on American eating habits. This film is appropriate for high school and adult audiences. It is available from Action for Children's Television, 46 Austin Street, Newtonville, Mass. 02160. Rental, $25; purchase, $185.

TV: The Anonymous Teacher. A fifteen-minute, 16mm color

film with sound that examines advertising, violence, and sexual and racial stereotyping on television. It includes commentary by noted researchers in the field of children's television. The film is appropriate for high school and adult audiences. It is distributed by Mass Media Ministries, 2116 N. Charles St., Baltimore, Md. 21218. Rental, $20; purchase, $225.